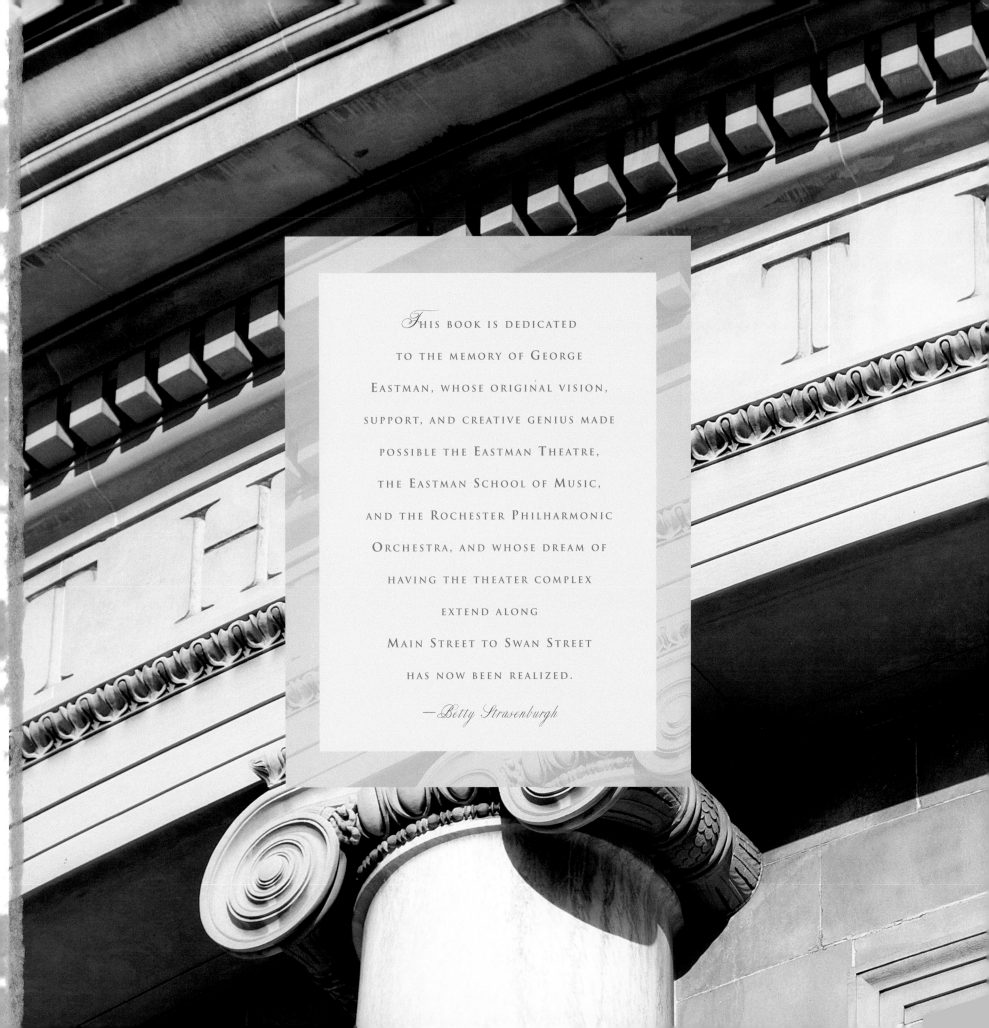

THIS BOOK IS DEDICATED
TO THE MEMORY OF GEORGE
EASTMAN, WHOSE ORIGINAL VISION,
SUPPORT, AND CREATIVE GENIUS MADE
POSSIBLE THE EASTMAN THEATRE,
THE EASTMAN SCHOOL OF MUSIC,
AND THE ROCHESTER PHILHARMONIC
ORCHESTRA, AND WHOSE DREAM OF
HAVING THE THEATER COMPLEX
EXTEND ALONG
MAIN STREET TO SWAN STREET
HAS NOW BEEN REALIZED.

—*Betty Strasenburgh*

Publisher: Rochester Philharmonic Orchestra, Inc.

Producer: Betty Strasenburgh

Project Manager: Suzanne Welch

Author: Elizabeth Brayer

Principal Photographer: Andy Olenick

Designer: Kathryn D'Amanda / Mill-Race Design Associates

Printer: Canfield & Tack

Library of Congress Control Number: 2010930128

ISBN 978-0-615-39373-5

Distributed by the Rochester Philharmonic Orchestra, Inc.

108 East Avenue, Rochester NY 14604, www.rpo.org

The Eastman Theatre

FULFILLING GEORGE EASTMAN'S DREAM

BY ELIZABETH BRAYER

WITH NEW PHOTOGRAPHY BY ANDY OLENICK

DESIGN
Kathryn D'Amanda

PROJECT MANAGEMENT
Suzanne Welch

Contents

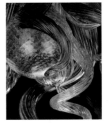

Author's Note

This book was a team effort. Once Betty Strasenburgh had chosen her team, we began working together and continue to be friends as we approach the three-year mark. We hope the result is not a "camel" as so many products of committees are.

Andy Olenick's photographic skills are especially evident in the breathtaking full-page and double-page spreads in the later chapters.

Kathryn D'Amanda's design talents are apparent on every page, and her design studio provided valuable space and inspiration.

Suzanne Welch was our project manager, keeping our records and keeping us on our toes. As chairman of the RPO board, she brought special expertise to those chapters.

We were fortunate that Rose-Marie Klipstein agreed to be our proofreader. In demand by many organizations, her contribution to this project was much appreciated.

David Peter Coppen of the Sibley Music Library worked tirelessly on our behalf to make the hundreds of photographs by Alexander Leventon and Lou Ouzer available. With Suzanne Welch, he tackled the daunting and time-consuming task of obtaining and recording permissions and copyrights. Every reasonable attempt has been made to identify the owners of copyrights. Errors or omissions will be corrected in subsequent editions.

Kathleen Connor, George Eastman House Legacy curator, put the impressive archives that she shepherds at our disposal.

Early on, the team decided that this would be a picture book. For more complete annotation of Part I, see my *George Eastman: A Biography* published by Johns Hopkins University Press. Chapters 6 and 7 in Part II are based in part on the two volumes of the history of the Eastman School of Music by Vincent Lenti published by the University of Rochester Press and on *Rochester's Orchestra 1922-1989* by William L. Cahn.

Chapter 8 is based on board minutes of the RPO and Eastman School of Music during the period after 1985, on notes kept by the informal group that met regularly during that time, and on interviews with some of those mentioned.

When did the Rochester Philharmonic Orchestra begin to be referred to by its acronym RPO? William Cahn tells us that while the term had been gradually coming into use, "September 1975 was the official starting date for…'RPO.' " We have attempted to follow that timeline wherever practical.

Elizabeth Brayer

PREFACE

The history of the Eastman Theatre is a complex and interesting one. It spans almost one hundred years. It is a story of individuals of vision and foresight—a story of community and institutional interactions—of cultural and civic philanthropy.

George Eastman gave to Rochester a treasure for all of us to enjoy. He built it for silent movies to be accompanied by an orchestra, but when "talkies" came, he supported the adaptation of the theater to a venue for musical performances.

My interest in the renovation and expansion of the theater comes from my experience as a student at the Eastman School of Music, my love for the Rochester Philharmonic Orchestra, and my interest in the East End neighborhood of the city, where I live.

George Eastman's original plan for the theater was for it to occupy the entire block from Gibbs Street to Swan Street. This plan was thwarted by the owner of one of the parcels of land, who would not sell at a reasonable price the lot at the corner of Main and Swan Streets. So Mr. Eastman decided to build the theater around the parcel he could not acquire. That accounts for the rather strange shape of the present theater. Years later the University of Rochester purchased this adjoining lot and turned it into a parking lot. Today the university, in building a new addition at this corner and renovating the original theater, is in effect finishing Eastman's original plan.

Mr. Eastman's interest in the theater project was so compelling, and the theater's subsequent history as a world-class musical venue is so noteworthy, that a book chronicling the story of the Eastman Theatre and the development of the changes that have been undertaken seemed not only appropriate, but necessary, to honor the men and women whose vision and hard work over many years made this civic treasure possible.

Special mention should also be given the late architect Robert Macon, who on his own, without being hired to do so and long before the present project was authorized, sketched plans for renovating the Eastman Theatre and the adjacent addition. These plans, thanks to the work of his partners Craig Jensen and Mike Stark, form the basis for most of the current renovations and expansion of the theater. Bob Macon started his career in the local architectural firm originally hired by George Eastman to design the theater. A day or two before he died in 2002, Bob asked his wife, Nancy, to package up these drawings and deliver them to me, in the hope that I would take on the completion of George Eastman's dream as a personal crusade.

This book project has been a great joy, not only to me as its instigator, but to the whole team who produced it: Betsy Brayer, author; Kathy D'Amanda, book designer; Andy Olenick, photographer; and Suzanne Welch, book project manager. To this group I owe many thanks.

Betty Strasenburgh

Part One

Music in Every Direction

The founding of the Eastman Theatre, the Eastman School of Music, and the Rochester Philharmonic Orchestra

What we do during our working hours determines what we have; what we do in our leisure hours determines what we are. —George Eastman

George Eastman's famous dictum became even more his own formula for living during the 1920s. He phrased it as a rhetorical question when discussing with a reporter his grand new music scheme and its connection to the gradual shortening of the work day: "What is going to be done with the leisure thus obtained? Do not imagine that I am a reformer—far from that. I am interested in music personally and I am led thereby, merely to want to share my pleasure with others." At a time when the five-day week was only a working-man's dream, Eastman saw it coming. He felt precious leisure would be wasted unless new forms of recreation were provided.

Those who shared in his pleasure could find the experience fatiguing. "GE is absolutely alcoholic about music," an exhausted Lillian Norton declared upon returning from a whirlwind visit to New York City. Twelve times in six days the trio of host plus "parson and parsonette," as Eastman called the rector of

An 1889 portrait photograph of George Eastman taken by the famous photographer known as Nadar

St. Paul's Episcopal Church and his wife, had trotted off to the opera and theater as well as to the Morgan Library and The Frick Collection. Twice they had trekked to the movies, and once they enjoyed a midnight supper at the Roosevelt Hotel. "The rest of the time we loafed," Eastman joked.

Lillian Norton, "parsonette" of St. Paul's Episcopal Church, was a frequent witness to Eastman's need to hear music.

Eastman reinforced Lillian Norton's metaphor when he said that same year:

> I am not a musician. I come pretty close to being a musical moron because I am unable to whistle a tune, to carry a tune, or remember a tune. But I love to listen to music and in listening I've come to think of it as a necessary part of life.… There are no drawbacks to music: you can't have too much of it. There is no residual bad effect like overindulgence in other things.

Later his young music school director Howard Hanson would describe in more lofty tones Eastman's latest project, that of combining a collegiate institution for talented musicians with a community school dedicated to musical training from childhood on, both supported by proceeds from the commercial

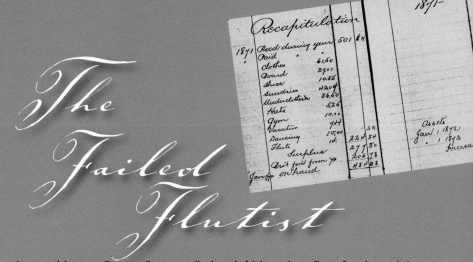

The Failed Flutist

booking of films: "Here indeed is the epic of the man who needed music, a man for whom music was a spiritual necessity, a man who believed that the entire community might be enriched by the art which had brought so much to him. Here, then, is his monument, the beautiful Eastman School of Music and Theatre, for the enrichment of community life. Long may they endure."

The other half of Eastman's great music project for Rochester which would "afford this community all of the benefits of music in every direction" stemmed from his belief that "the trouble with this country is that it has too few listeners. There are probably enough performers already," he said shortly after the Eastman School opened and began adding to the ranks of performers. The schooling of listeners "must start with school children," he vowed. And so when the director of music in the public schools came [in 1918]…and said: "Mr. Eastman, the city is willing to furnish all the teachers that are required but it is difficult, if not impossible, in the present state of the city finances, to get appropriations for band and orchestra instruments.…Will you help out?" he was ready with a check for $15,000 that provided 250 band and orchestra instruments. The instruments would be owned by "the School of Music, which is about to be affiliated with the Rochester University." Eastman realized that "these bands and orchestras in the public schools are primarily to produce performers but they also are powerful influences in training and interesting listeners."

Two questions continue to intrigue. First, just how tone deaf was Eastman? He loved to foster that impression and, generally, everyone agreed with him. Once the Eastman School was opened, he bragged to have flunked the tests used as part of the entrance examination. And when invited to join a "company of music sharks" in New York City, he declared he "should not dare to mix up with them."

At age thirteen, George Eastman (below left) bought a flute for three dollars and spent the next two years learning to play *Annie Laurie*—badly. A second flute was purchased three years later in 1871, this one for fourteen dollars as Eastman's neat and carefully executed ledger for 1871 shows (above).

But his performing abilities did not improve and forty-eight years later, he decided to concentrate his fortune and hands-on efforts on training listeners as well as performers.

Years later, Eastman's neighbor George D. B. Bonbright (right) grumbled, "The trouble with you, George, is that you should have learned to play the banjo. No girl would marry a man who plays the flute as badly as you do."

Even now with all of my musical experience I find great difficulty distinguishing a sonata from a violin, or the cello from
a scherzo; when I am with musical people I try to get them
to converse on hog raising or alfalfa growing. That of course
is when I am away from home. The very nice bunch that we
have gathered here know all about my shortcomings and they
do not waste their time trying to talk music with me.

Second, at what point did Eastman fully commit himself to
create the Theatre and School of Music? Was it 1918 when Eastman bought the Institute of Musical Art and presented it to
the University of Rochester for use as a music school? Or earlier in December 1916 when Charles Thoms, the real estate
agent who had sold Eastman the Marvin Culver farm on which
900 East Avenue, Eastman's Rochester home, would rise, suggested a music hall on the very spot where the Eastman
Theatre and School of Music would be built three years later?

"What would you think of a project to build a Music Hall in
Rochester?" inquired Thoms. "Our people are becoming very
fond of music, due in large measure to the Dossenbach Orchestra, which you have sustained so generously. Rochester has some
fine moving picture houses," Thoms argued, "but no adequate
Auditorium in which to listen to a first class concert, either vocal
or instrumental.... We have what we think is an ideal location…on Gibbs Street…fronting on two streets…." Even if the
thought had not yet occurred to Eastman, which is unlikely,
Thoms had put together an intriguing package for Eastman to
mull over. "One hundred subscribers would build the whole
thing," Thoms concluded. Or, one person could build the hall
and the subscribers could support the orchestra, which is the
way it would happen.

Antecedents

As early as 1915, organist and choral conductor George Barlow
Penny, a founder in 1910 of the Rochester Conservatory of Music,
which was not an accredited school but a merging of piano,
voice, theory, and violin lessons, told his orchestration class
that George Eastman was going to build a new school of music.
(Penny would continue on the faculty of the Eastman School.)
Since neither Thoms nor Penny was an intimate of Eastman,
how they knew is hard to determine. Most probably it was just
in the air, a rumor based on Eastman's intense interest in music
for his own personal enjoyment, combined with the extrava-
gant largesse of his civic-minded gifts to Rochester, which were
already out-pacing anything previously given to the city.

Perhaps he was thinking about it even earlier in the century,
when he installed his giant theater organ and began regular
music programs in his home, financially supported the summer program of music in the parks, or helped mop up the
deficits incurred by local orchestral groups. In 1904 University

of Rochester president Rush Rhees had architects draw up a master plan for the university campus that included a music school. All Rhees needed was to find the right donor, and it is possible he had Eastman in mind from the beginning.

Perhaps Hermann Dossenbach, violinist and conductor, planted the seed. In 1911 Eastman and nine others formed a Musical Council for Rochester, the first act of which was to send Dossenbach to Berlin for a year of study. From there he wrote to Eastman: "I feel as you do, that the most pleasing Quartettes are the Haydn, Mozart and Shuberts [sic] also the early Quartettes of Beethoven." Those who insist that the only music Eastman liked was Wagnerian have not noticed such passages.

When Dossenbach returned "to resume his baton with the inspiration and enthusiasm of a year's study in Europe" behind him, a committee of nine guarantors—chairman Rhees, Eastman, and Hiram Watson Sibley the largest underwriters—completely reorganized Dossenbach's "orchestral enterprise." Their program declared: "The orchestra will consist of sixty players, for the most part professional musicians from Rochester and will bear the name The Rochester Orchestra." Six concerts a season were scheduled at the Lyceum Theatre; soloists included David Hochstein and Efrem Zimbalist on the violin, and John Adams Warner, son of architect J. Foster Warner, on the piano. In these same early years, Eastman helped pick up the deficit for the Symphony Orchestra, founded about 1901 as a group of amateurs and students who performed free concerts, usually in the spacious auditoriums of the East and West High Schools. Ludwig Schenck, violinist and composer, who would go on to play in the Eastman Theatre Orchestra and Rochester Philharmonic Orchestra, was its conductor. Eastman also subscribed to concerts by the Community Chorus and concerts sponsored by the Tuesday Musicale, a group founded by cultivated ladies about 1890.

Music had been part of the Rochester scene since public concerts were held in the Eagle Tavern in the 1820s. German immigrants brought their musical traditions. Jenny Lind was one of the visiting European artists who gave recitals in the commodious Corinthian Hall which opened in 1849. Amateur orchestral ensembles and choral societies flourished during the nineteenth century and culminated in the first Rochester Philharmonic Orchestra, which existed from 1865 until the mid-1880s.

Eastman's Milieu

Eastman's grand project, which appeared to many Rochesterians to be the culmination of a century's growing concern for music in the community, may have germinated during the 1890s when Eastman first organized trips to opera in New York, attended musicales in London at the home of the Kodak Ltd. manager whose wife, Josephine Dickman, was a trained singer. He bought Aeolian pianos and organs with their canned music for his Rochester house and North Carolina retreat. He was unable to play himself, but thought, according to Murray Bartlett, rector of St. Paul's, that "it was the proper thing to have in the house, and somebody might want to play it." So Eastman bought a selection of records and sheet music; "not much popular music," Bartlett said, "because he realized, as far as I can see, that he liked good music and he wanted to like good music. He couldn't carry a tune [but] anything I could say about music helped him." About 1898 Bartlett started taking dinner with Eastman every Sunday until his marriage in 1903. Bartlett could listen to the player organ and did so "every Sunday afternoon for one-half to an hour, before other people arrived. The next thing was," Bartlett recalled, "he wanted to build his house and he wanted to have an organ built in it." When Eastman heard that a man named Hammond of Buffalo had put an organ in his house, he asked Bartlett and Beecher Aldrich, the organist at St. Paul's, to go with him to see this

organ. "Aldrich tried out the organ," Bartlett recalled. "Of course it sounded better when played by an organist. George was very much impressed," and an organ for Eastman's home was assured. Bartlett gave his friend one more little shove: horrified that Eastman had a male quartet sing along when he invited people to hear the organ, he gave him a book on chamber music for Christmas. Gradually Eastman agreed that the string quartet or piano quintet was better for the house than the organ and by the 1920s the organ was used mainly at breakfast.

Murray Bartlett (right), rector of St.Paul's, listened to recorded music on the player organ at Eastman's home on Sunday afternoons.

REV. MURRAY BARTLETT

A new social elite was created by Eastman when he made up guest lists composed of his business associates and employees, some of the leaders of the older society, the bright young physicians and surgeons recruited for the medical school that Eastman founded in 1920, and the wonderful international stew of Britons, Russians, Scandinavians, French, and Americans that began to bubble up when the Eastman School of Music really got under way.

The Eastman School of Music had many conventional precedents in the music conservatories of nineteenth century America, but the Eastman Theatre, a financial as well as artistic marriage of his two loves, music and film, was pure George Eastman. In that era silent movies were regularly accompanied by a theater organ and sometimes a movie orchestra—but only Eastman begot a scheme whereby showings of movies in a cavernous 3,300-seat auditorium were mandated to financially support a symphony orchestra regularly playing serious music. "If only it had worked," Howard Hanson sighed later. "Think of the symphony orchestras across the country which could have been thus supported…. What we're up against today is the problem of needing a George Eastman—as could every city with a philharmonic orchestra."

All of these influences serve to belie the bilious critic who wrote, upon the opening of the Eastman School of Music in 1921, that here was "the world's greatest experiment in attempting to exchange money for culture." Much more than money was involved. But despite portents and rumors, few knew about the music school gestating in Eastman's mind; indeed, his secretive ways led even a University of Rochester historian to write in the 1970s: "Out of a clear sky, apparently,

The Dossenbach Quintette at Oak Lodge

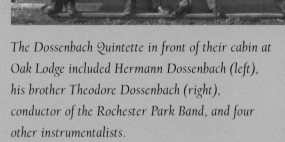

In 1900 Hermann Dossenbach, violinist and conductor, put together a group of experienced players as the small orchestra bearing his name. From the beginning, the Dossenbach Orchestra was plagued by financial troubles, and Eastman was one of a group of music lovers who picked up the annual deficit. In a manner reminiscent of aristocratic Europe, Dossen-

The Dossenbach Quintette in front of their cabin at Oak Lodge included Hermann Dossenbach (left), his brother Theodore Dossenbach (right), conductor of the Rochester Park Band, and four other instrumentalists.

bach began playing for Eastman at least as early as February 1902, presumably as a soloist, as his fee for services was $20. After the move to the mansion in 1905, Eastman drew a "Quintette" from Dossenbach's Orchestra to play formal programs of chamber music Sunday and Wednesday evenings for the next fifteen years. (On evenings when quartet music was played, the Dossenbach Quintette obligingly became the Dossenbach Quartet.) By regularly employing these musicians, Eastman was also further subsidizing the Rochester Orchestra. Over the years the Dossenbach groups were transported to Oak Lodge in North Carolina by their own railroad car and housed in a special cabin with practice room and bunk room. Other times, when the patron was on vacation, he picked up the tab for the Quintette to play for Rochester or out-of-town friends such as the Albrights, donors of the present-day Albright-Knox Art Gallery in Buffalo.

Early Musical Influences

Clockwise from upper left: Josephine Dickman, George Dickman, Mary Mulligan with George Eastman, Edward Mulligan

Beginning in the 1890s, Eastman's friends on both sides of the Atlantic fanned his love for music. Josephine Dickman, wife of Kodak's UK manager, was a trained singer who often performed for Kodak Ltd. Entertainments. The Dickmans held regular evening musicales at their home in Hampstead, where George Eastman was often in attendance. About 1896, Eastman began employing Hermann Dossenbach to lead evening musicales at his East Avenue home. Soon thereafter, he bought a pump and player organ for his home. Rochester neighbor Mary Mulligan, wife of Eastman's surgeon, member of the Tuesday Musicale and frequent hostess in Eastman's home ("King George and Queen Mary of the Palace," critics sneered), took him in hand on this side of the Atlantic. More perplexing is the role of the mystifying Susan Brown who, Gertrude Strong Achilles tells us, left Rochester in the 1880s to study music in Europe because there was no conservatory in Rochester, having been sent off with a bunch of violets from young George Eastman. Susan triumphantly waltzed into Eastman's home in the late 1920s. Gertrude theorized that the founding of the Eastman School of Music was in direct response to his losing track of this early love.

Emily Sibley Watson and her son James Averell

Mr. Eastman inquired of Dr. Rhees, in 1918, whether he would like to have a school of music affiliated with the university. It seems evident that the President had previously been lukewarm regarding a professional school in both music and law."

Despite his instructions to campus architects to include a music building on the 1904 master plan, Rhees admitted that the realization of such plans was "somewhat in the future." For years he had been resistant to suggestions of a music school without endowment or academic standards. A master at matching the buildings he wanted with the right donors, Rhees had already fit his wish for an art gallery to Emily Sibley Watson's desire to memorialize her architect son, James Averell. But the Memorial Art Gallery of the University of Rochester was given in 1912 as a building only, without endowment for operations or acquisitions. Rhees was anxious to avoid repeating this with a music school. In linking music to the memory of his mother, Eastman became uncharacteristically willing to "spend money like water," as Rhees later described the process.

The Institute of Musical Art

One element that brought matters to a head was the financial plight of Rochester's chief music school. The Institute of Musical Art was founded in 1913 in a house adjacent to the university campus, by Hermann Dossenbach and Alf Klingenberg, a Norwegian pianist who had been trained in Germany. "DKG" was prefixed to the institute in 1914 when Oscar Gareissen, voice teacher and recital soloist, joined the original partners. Then in 1915 the institute consolidated further with the Rochester Conservatory of Music, whose director, George Barlow Penny, was among those agitating for a university-sponsored school of music in Rochester. Rhees was a board member of the institute. Students and faculty members included Arthur See, a musician crippled from polio, who would become the secretary-manager of the Eastman School of Music, and Hinda Rosenblum [Miller], the mother of the future world-famous musician Mitch Miller, who would himself be a product of the Eastman School of Music. See's first glimpse of Eastman was disappointing: One warm summer evening, Eastman sat in a cool hallway of the institute listening to the music through the open French doors. "That's George Eastman," whispered Mrs. Klingenberg, and young See, expecting a giant radiating power, was much let down by the spare man he saw who exuded insignificance. "You could pass him on the street a thousand times and never notice him." See would learn that Eastman's power was clothed in somber garments; from the 1950s he would recall Eastman as the cold and cruel tyrant who fired Hermann Dossenbach, Arthur Alexander, Alf Klingenberg, and Eric Thacher Clarke for little or no apparent reason.

In 1917, with Klingenberg as director, the institute faced increasing financial difficulties with its provisional charter from the state's Board of Regents due to expire the next year.

NEW PLAN FOR INSTITUTE OF MUSIC

Building of Institute at No. 47 Prince Street.

Provided contributions of not less than 2,500 a year for five years are obtained, George Eastman has offered to purchase the property now housing the Institute of Musical Art, No. 47 Prince street, the institution to be chartered by the regents of the University of the State of New York. Mr. Eastman would present the property to the trustees of the new corporation, in which no trustee or other individual would hold stock or have any proprietory interest.

The contributions asked by Mr. East- man would supplement for the support of an educational musical institution the income from pupils. Another provision stipulates that Alf Klingenberg, the present director, remain as director and teacher of piano for not less than five years.

Through co-operation with the University of Rochester, it is said, the usual four-year course would be enlarged by the addition of college subjects.

Announcement of further details will be made soon.

Taking matters into her own hands, the brash and direct Mrs. Klingenberg called upon George Eastman without appointment, managing to gain access to his office and inveigle a contribution from him. In April 1918, following a conference with Rhees, Eastman purchased the school and its equipment for $28,000, in order, as Rhees phrased it, "that a new corpo-

Upon purchase of the Institute of Musical Art, Eastman and Rhees agreed to retain its director, Alf Klingenberg (below), a Norwegian pianist who had been trained in Germany, for five years.

Eastman, seen here in 1910, was viewed by Arthur See as a cold, cruel tyrant who fired Hermann Dossenbach, Arthur Alexander, Alf Klingenberg, and Eric Thacher Clarke for little or no apparent reason.

Eastman soon decided that the quaint Queen Anne house would never do as Rochester's music center. Adding a codicil to his will in July 1918, he advised his niece, Ellen Dryden, that "the proper disposition of the house and lot at 900 East Avenue…with fixtures and such furnishings as you do not want…would be to give it to the University of Rochester for a music school…. I shall rely upon you to carry out this plan." At what point he began to think that he "wanted to see the action during my lifetime," and that he would therefore undertake a "project to build a Music Hall in Rochester" is not clear. Indications are that between the purchase of the institute and 12 December 1918 when Rhees had the university's state charter amended to allow for establishing a professional music school, he deliberated and conversed with Rhees and others until a master plan gradually evolved. Perhaps the codicil to that ever-changing will was just to make sure the project went ahead in case he died suddenly before a new school could be built.

On 14 February 1919, Eastman wrote to a vacationing Rhees that "things concerning the Music School have been moving quite rapidly." From Oak Lodge Eastman had lined up former architect, former mayor, inventor of the mail chute, and now

ration may be organized to operate the Institute in the interest of musical education in Rochester, any profits accruing from the operation…to be turned back into the Institute for the improvement of its work." Also at that first private talk, Eastman and Rhees agreed only that the real estate title would be vested in the university, which would place it at the disposal of the Institute of Musical Art free of rental charges. It also called for Alf Klingenberg to remain as director for five years.

Music at Home

On the home front, Eastman was doing his bit to buck up the music situation, too. He had finished enlarging his conservatory in September 1919, installed a second organ, and hired a music director, New Zealander Arthur Alexander, for a $10,000 retainer (a hefty sum for a musician in those days). Eastman had directed Alexander to oversee the music at Eastman's house and help at the Institute of Musical Art, but secretly Eastman had larger plans for the young musician. As he told Rhees on 14 February 1919:

> The proposition is to make an offer to Alexander…assuming that it will take another year beyond that to get the hall into operation …. [It would take more than three more years.] All so far are agreed that it would be a much more interesting experiment to have a new man like Alexander tackle the job than a man who had already made a reputation as a director…. He is enamored with Rochester and is crazy about leading an orchestra…. If he connects up with us he will spend both summers in England studying under Beecham.

This meant, of course, that Dossenbach was out. The "one fundamental and unchangeable purpose of the great musical project which has been undertaken here in Rochester," as Eastman called it in a talk he delivered to the founders of the Subscribers Association one evening in his own living room, "is to afford this community all of the benefits of music in every direction." His plan included "offering Mr. Dossenbach the leadership of the movie orchestra, with the understanding that he could not in any event become the leader of the big orchestra." In the end Dossenbach turned down the position of conductor of the movie orchestra. One can only guess that in his mind "perfectly willing to work in harmony" was not the same thing as "being under" Alexander.

realtor James G. Cutler to get options on some properties centrally located in the city, particularly for those traveling by trolley. When he got home, he had his own architects, Gordon & Kaelber, "draw up some floor plans [to see] if the lot would accommodate everything we need." When he saw that it did, he gave Cutler "directions to take the property."

Among the properties acquired was an imposing brick structure with beamed ceilings owned by Edward and Mary Mulligan. Eastman paid his physician $60,000 for the property and soon received a note from "Ed" to take back $10,000 of the purchase price and apply it to a music school scholarship in the name of the Mulligans' daughter, Molly.

In February 1919 Cutler and Hermann Dossenbach called at Kodak Office to say that at the urging of Rhees an underwriting committee headed by Rochester businessman George W. Todd had been formed to "sell the seats for the 1919-1920 orchestra concerts and asked if the plan was agreeable to me. I told them I had some plans affecting the musical situation here that were not quite ready to disclose but might have a bearing on what should be done for the orchestra and that I would be able to talk about it in a few days." Shortly afterward, the *Democrat & Chronicle* announced publicly for the first time that George Eastman planned to build "a Concert Hall and School of Music…surpassed by no other in the world."

Eastman had finished enlarging his conservatory in September 1919, installed a second organ, and hired a music director, New Zealander Arthur Alexander (left), for a $10,000 retainer (a hefty sum for a musician in those days). Eastman had directed Alexander to oversee the music at Eastman's house and help at the Institute of Musical Art, but secretly Eastman had larger plans for the young musician.

Sibley Music Library

In organizing a major new music conservatory, an adequate library is a major priority, and fortunately, a distinguished musical library was already in the possession of the university. It was augmented by works already at the DKG Institute, some orchestral music purchased from Dossenbach, and the works Eastman was able to locate in Europe through his never-fail agent, Joseph Thacher Clarke. In 1904 Elbert Newton, a Rochester church organist, had discussed the need for a library of music compositions and publications with Hiram Watson Sibley, son of a founder and the first president of Western Union Hiram Sibley, who at his death in 1888 was the wealthiest man in the Genesee Valley. The younger Sibley, brother to Emily Sibley Watson and a collector in various categories of objects ranging from ivories to paintings to armor, was interested and commissioned Newton to begin hunting down the standard works of music which in the end came to about 8,000 volumes. The collection was housed for the next seventeen years in Sibley Hall, which the elder Sibley had built on the Prince Street campus of the University of Rochester, and was open to the citizens of Rochester. Spacious new quarters were prepared in 1921 in the new Eastman School of Music to accommodate the library, which even then Eastman was able to describe as "the third or fourth largest musical library in the United States."

Rhees described an avalanche of gifts descending upon the library once plans for the new school were revealed. So many gifts were received that the cataloguers could not keep up and a moratorium had to be called until it could be determined what was needed. Many arrived unsolicited on Eastman's doorstep from Dr. Leon Lilienfeld, a Viennese chemist who had been puttering along for decades with a Kodak film process but who also helped import Kilbourn Quartet musicians such as Joseph Press and Vladimir Resnikoff. (The musicians were guided through customs by Kodak men in New York who spoke German, one instance of many of the whole organization being called upon to participate in Eastman's projects.) In the years following World War I, Sibley and his surrogates visited libraries and museums in Germany to purchase many rare manuscripts for the Sibley Library.

In 1925 Hiram Watson Sibley gave $50,000 toward the expansion of his library, particularly earmarked for rare musical manuscripts. Barbara Duncan, brought to Rochester from the Boston Public Library in 1921 to serve as librarian, sought out libraries, orchestral scores, and publications and generally haunted library sales and auctions. Sibley died the same year as Eastman, 1932, and like his sister Emily but unlike Eastman, he left no endowment to support what he had started. Yet as a result of all these efforts and sources, the Sibley Music Library is now the largest academic music collection in the Americas. In 1937 a separate structure was built on Swan Street to house the collection—the first music library in the United States to have its own building. In 1989 a new block-long, $18 million building called Eastman Place opened with the library occupying part of the second, third, and fourth floors.

The original Kilbourn Quartet as seen in an early issue of The Note Book, a student publication of the Eastman School of Music

Librarian Barbara Duncan

Separate from the deliberate combing of the world to assemble music for the Sibley Library was the mad scramble to get the contemporary popular scores needed for the movie orchestra. Here the practical Eastman emerged again. As he wrote Raymond Ball, university treasurer: "Don't you think it would be a good plan to get some stamps 'The Property of the Eastman Theatre' and stamp all the music which we purchase?… I understand there is liable to be pilfering…. The stamps…should have a distinctive design so the mere shape would disclose the identity."

It amazed many people that a man who had such a renowned ability for grasping the larger essentials could handle details with equal facility—and could spare the time for them. After the theater was finished, Eastman hovered over it with relentless devotion. If he was not actually present, the possibility that he might arrive suddenly kept all on their toes. In a sense he is still there: every mural, marble block, and chandelier is a reminder of his meticulous supervision.

A Musical Expert for Europe

Eastman decided that Joseph Thacher Clarke, his long-time patent expert for Europe, cultural mentor, old cycling companion, highly effective "head hunter," and on occasion, industrial spy, could also be his "musical expert for Europe" and negotiate for the purchase of libraries of orchestral scores. Clarke was in Paris on Eastman's musical library mission when he took sick and died in September 1920. One of the great Kodak characters thus passed from the scene.

Kilbourn Hall

In contrast to the 3,300-seat Eastman Theatre's lavish magnificence was an exquisite, intimate, and delicate auditorium that would be the setting for chamber music. Accommodating 450, Eastman called it Kilbourn Hall, a remembrance of his mother, Maria Kilbourn Eastman, and intended it as the central feature of the school. Intimacy rather than grandeur would be stressed, the donor said, "so that the attention of the listener would

Winter was such a perfectionist that he mounted the scaffolding himself to affix the finishing touches.

As the opening of Kilbourn Hall on 3 March 1922 approached, Eastman and others came to the hall to check out the sound: "The Quartet made a trial of the acoustics…and some of the critics thought the room was a little too resonant and others thought it a little too dead. I [Eastman] heard them play this morning and concluded, with a number of others, that the acoustics appear to be perfect. No difference can be detected in any of the seats."

Ellen Dryden (above), Eastman's niece

Eastman hung animal trophies from his Rocky Mountain and African hunting trips in the spacious second floor corridor (right) between the theater and music school.

not be distracted from the music by too assertive decoration." The color schemes for the two auditoriums were supervised by Ezra Winter, an artist of national reputation, who was also awarded the contract for the painted frieze and decorative scheme for the ceiling. Thomas B. Wadelton, who had done Eastman's dining room in 1905, created the paneled ceiling in Kilbourn Hall under the direction of McKim Mead & White.

Eastman continued to keep close tabs on all aspects of his musical complex, flooding the mailboxes of employees Arthur See, Clarence Livingston, and Gertrude Vayo with directives (written with his favorite green pencil that he carried in his vest pocket), and in general running the school and theater the way he ran the Eastman Kodak Company. "At the next concert," he wrote Miss Vayo in November 1922, "I would like to have the

Accommodating 450, Eastman named the auditorium Kilbourn Hall, in remembrance of his mother, Maria Kilbourn Eastman. He intended it as the central feature of the school. Intimacy rather than grandeur would be stressed, he said, "so that the attention of the listener would not be distracted from the music by too assertive decoration."

Opening Night of Kilbourn Hall...

A small portrait of Maria Kilbourn East-man, her son's favorite, which had been painted from life years earlier by Rochester artist Robert MacCameron, was hung on the stage for the opening night of Kilbourn Hall 4 March 1922. As he wrote his old partner Henry Strong's daughter, Gertrude Strong Achilles, "Outside of a very few members of the family there is nobody I should like so much to have present as you and Helen, old associations are so strong." Helen Strong Carter (with her sister Gertrude, the donor of Strong Memorial Hospital) did attend

after she received a plea: "Can't you manage it? I want Mother's old friends more than anybody else." So did his niece, Ellen Dryden.

curtain closed until say two minutes before the concert begins. The footlights should be on while the curtain is closed so as to get the effect of the beautiful coloring of the curtain. If this trial proves satisfactory continue the practice." He then instructed her to put a notice in the program to the effect that "The audience is invited to promenade in the second story corridor after the music. A collection of pictures from the Memorial Art Gallery is on view."

Eastman had arranged with the director of the university's art gallery to provide loan exhibitions of American paintings for the spacious second floor corridor. He would hang animal trophies, as well, from his Rocky Mountain and African hunting trips and give informal tours to the Preparatory Department students who came to the Eastman School afternoons for their music lessons. More and more he was retiring from business and devoting a major portion of his time to personally running the music show. "You will no doubt be surprised to know that I am contemplating quitting Kodak to accept a professorship in harmony in a new school," he quipped to a friend.

You will no doubt be surprised to know that I am contemplating quitting Kodak to accept a professorship in harmony in a new school!

—*George Eastman*

THEATER ORGANS

Practical as well as aesthetic matters engaged Eastman's steel-trap mind and attention to detail. One goal was to have his music school "mark the highest development in America in musical equipment." Apparently none of Klingenberg's equipment was used; the organ from the old Institute of Musical Art, for example, was sold to a church in New Hampshire, and between November 1920 and July 1923 eighteen new organs were purchased, including thirteen practice organs, three teaching organs, and an organ for the theater and Kilbourn Hall. Costs ranged from $3,500 for a practice organ to $78,705 for the grand theater organ of more than 10,000 pipes and 140 stops built by the Austin Organ Company of Hartford, Connecticut.

Harold Gleason, Eastman's personal organist, engaged four organ consultants "who examined and gave written opinions of the specifications for the Theatre and Kilbourn Hall organs." Gleason himself

The Austin Organ
IN THE
EASTMAN THEATRE, ROCHESTER, N. Y.
The largest theatre organ ever built.

THE CONSOLE

AUSTIN ORGAN COMPANY
HARTFORD, CONN.

The Austin Organ was reported to be the largest theater organ in the world at the time of construction. The eight divisions, all really separate organs, each larger than the average church or theater organ, were Great, Swell, Choir, Solo, Orchestral, Echo, String, and Pedal. Weighing forty-five tons, its electric circuits used several thousand miles of wire; the largest pipe was thirty-two feet tall and weighed over 400 pounds. "The console is mounted on an elevator and turnstile and can be moved from orchestra pit to stage as desired," the *Post-Express* reported. "This console [also] controls and plays a grand piano by means of a movable player placed over the piano keys."

Harold Gleason (left and below), Eastman's personal organist, became head of the organ department at the Eastman School of Music. Gleason engaged four organ consultants "who examined and gave written opinions of the specifications for the Theatre and Kilbourn Hall organs."

traveled to inspect organs in Oberlin, the Wanamaker store in Philadelphia, to organ manufacturers Skinner, Austin, Wurlitzer, and Möller, and attended the Northeast Conservatory class in Motion Picture Playing. Joseph Bonnet, the famous French organist engaged to teach at the school, was scheduled to dedicate the Skinner organ in Kilbourn Hall in mid-April 1922; when Skinner did not deliver on time, he heard from Eastman: "Your failure to have the organ ready before Mr. Bonnet sails for France is not only a disappointment to us but will cause a large financial loss and this is to notify you that I shall hold you responsible."

The theater organs, Eastman wrote proudly, "are two of the most important instruments built thus far representing the latest and most comprehensive thought of modern organ engineering and musical development.... The Austin organ was situated back stage in an ideal position "for most of our work," Eastman told a consultant on 5 December 1925, "but when we want to compel people to stick cotton in their ears it is not quite loud enough."

A studio in the theater was equipped with a Wurlitzer orchestral organ with all modern instrumental equivalents and complete facilities for screening pictures. Eastman particularly liked the rising platform idea for the organ and orchestra, which he copied from the Hippodrome in New York, because it eliminated the confusion of players filing in and taking their seats.

He foresaw the "comparatively new profession" of theater organist emerging and so had a circular prepared about a course in "Organ Accompanying of Motion Pictures" which would be taught by his own theater organists who were, he noted, "past masters of the art they teach." The organists had to be improvisers and quick change artists of the first order, continually scoring a new and comprehensive weekly program. With such an investment in the giant theater organ, plus another Wurlitzer organ in the projection room, and a class in theater organ playing in the offing, it is no wonder that Eastman chose to ignore the coming of "talkies" and was crushed when they took over and put theater organs and indeed his whole wonderful theater complex out of business.

Besides ordering those eighteen organs and one hundred pianos, Eastman sent up to Sibley's department store for two hundred wastebaskets. He then positioned each wastebasket for maximum efficiency so that wherever the occupant of the studio or office was seated, he or she could toss the waste and hit the basket without getting up. If Eastman saw a wastebasket in the wrong place during his weekly inspection trip, he would reposition it. His neatness compelled him to pick up a program a thoughtless person had dropped, and as a detail that could not be left undone, he conducted a thorough search for

To the most wonderful Music
School in America. Long may
its flag wave.

George Gershwin.

It should come as no surprise that 18 organs, 100 pianos, and 200 wastebaskets were among the first things Eastman ordered for his new music school. This is probably Howard Hanson's office/studio (left) with two pianos and the corporate photographic portrait of Eastman on the wall.

George Gershwin, who came to Rochester in 1925 to conduct his new Rhapsody in Blue, *inscribed in a large, bold hand (above): "To the most wonderful Music School in America. Long may its flag wave." Gershwin's inscription included the now famous clarinet glissando and solo that opens* Rhapsody in Blue.

a non-rustling paper for the programs. "The overheating of the Hall has been complained of," he wrote superintendent Clarence Livingston, while Gertrude Vayo was told to "let me know whenever you observe the thermometer going above 70, giving me the day and hour and the location of the thermometer." But this near-obsessive attention to detail paid off, as is indicated by two comments in the theater's guest book:

Australian soprano Nellie Melba, a house guest of Eastman's during her stay wrote, "To me it is a most beautiful fairy tale—which will live for ever," while George Gershwin, who came to Rochester in 1925 to conduct his new *Rhapsody in Blue* inscribed in a large, bold hand: "To the most wonderful Music School in America. Long may its flag wave."

One of his greatest interests was the careful scrutiny of these plans, which very often resulted in important changes. —Marion Folsom

In George Eastman's outer office was a large flat cabinet of the kind found in an architect's office—full of blueprints for buildings planned, currently under construction, or recently erected. "One of his greatest interests," wrote Marion Folsom, Eastman's administrative assistant in the 1920s who would later be the Secretary of Health, Education and Welfare in the Eisenhower cabinet, "was the careful scrutiny of these plans, which very often resulted in important changes." From his post, Folsom heard such comments as, "I don't like the way the draftsman makes his Rs." If he had been born in more affluent circumstances, it is possible that Eastman would have pursued architecture as a career.

Enter McKim, Mead & White

Even as an amateur, Eastman was an inspired contributor to factory architecture, one of the great unheralded and unrecorded contributions of America to the history of world

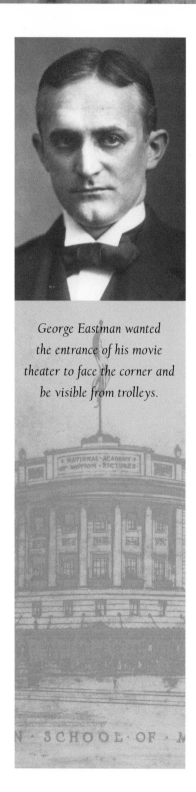

George Eastman wanted the entrance of his movie theater to face the corner and be visible from trolleys.

architecture. He may never have heard of Louis Sullivan (although one of his architects, Claude Bragdon, wrote extensively about Sullivan), but he certainly adhered to Sullivan's famous dictum "Form follows function" for factory buildings and pragmatic projects such as the School of Medicine and Dentistry of the University of Rochester. For more aesthetic projects, such as his mansion or the Eastman Theatre and School of Music, he employed nationally known "slipcover" architects after he and a local architect had worked out the plans and the program. Then if an academically trained Beaux Arts architect wanted to add a fancy cornice or Gothic tower to hide the elevator shaft, that was all right as long as it did not interfere with the plan and if costs were kept in check.

"What has happened in the matter of the School of Music?" inquired architect Burt Fenner of his former colleagues at the Rochester firm of Gordon & Kaelber in July 1919. "We are all much interested in knowing whether it is going ahead." Fenner, a native Rochesterian, was with the nationally prominent firm of McKim, Mead & White, whose man on the job he had been during the construction of Eastman's house, 1902-1905, but he kept in chatty touch with his Rochester acquaintances in hopes that the famous New York firm would land another Eastman project. By 1919 Charles McKim had died, Stanford White had been murdered, and William Rutherford Mead had retired to Maine, where he remained in close

· EASTMAN · SCHOOL · OF · MUSIC · U · OF · R · ROCHESTER · N · Y ·

consultation with his old firm, the principals of which now included Lawrence Grant White, Stanford's son. The Eastman Theatre and School of Music would be Larry White's first major project, and he was determined to make it a showcase success.

Fenner learned to his dismay that "Mr. Eastman, with local architects Ed Gordon and Will Kaelber, has been at work since February over plans. They have visited theaters and music halls all the way from Boston to the Mississippi River," Fenner wrote to senior sage Mead, "and have gotten all the practical details of the auditorium construction worked out to the last inch, but the result is an abominable plan which is architecturally impossible. If they had only gotten us into it at the start," Fenner

sniffed, "I am sure we could have saved the situation." But Fenner was still "satisfied that we can revise the plan so as to make it architecturally possible and at the same time meet all the practical requirements."

Having determined that the modest Queen Anne house of the Institute of Musical Art was not suitable for his grand plans and that he did not want to wait until his own demise turned his mansion into a music school and thus miss the fun of planning and building, Eastman had gone looking for suitable lots. By the summer of 1919, he had selected a site near the one which real estate agent Charles Thoms had suggested in 1916 during the height of speculation that

28

On 3 November 1919, Gibbs Street was a quiet residential street; but George Eastman had just purchased all the residences. By 8 November, the houses were quickly being demolished. This one still has porch furniture and curtains in the windows.

Two months after the houses on Gibbs Street were demolished, an enormous hole was dug to receive the school and theater. Prominently, the apartment building that occupied the corner of Main and Swan Streets would remain.

an Eastman music hall was in the offing. It was, Eastman agreed, the most attractive one available—several blocks east of the business district on Main Street itself and a half-mile west of the university campus. Best of all, it was on a trolley line.

Coincidentally, the area was once a grove of trees near which Eastman had climbed George Selden's attic stairs for lessons in wet plate photography. Surveying the sylvan scene in the 1870s, the bank clerk had pronounced it worthy of a painter's palette; forty years later the grove was nearly gone and in its place, spanning Main Street, stood a pleasant residential neighborhood of turn-of-the-century frame houses and a 1910 apartment building. Buying up the houses proved to be no problem, but the owner of the apartments demanded what Eastman consid-

ered an exorbitant price, and so, refusing to pay the "baksheesh," he had Will Kaelber redraw the plans for the large auditorium so that it fit the remaining trapezoidal plot.

A Skewed Axis

Most important was positioning the grand entrance on the very corner of the plot, which was not a right but an oblique angle. Eastman saw this wide sweep as ideal for a marquee and entrance to be seen by both street car riders on Main Street and motorists there and on Grove and Gibbs Streets. But the positioning automatically skewed "the axis of the auditorium at an angle which is not a right angle to the most important façade," and this is what so bothered McKim, Mead & White. "Architecturally it is extremely difficult to obtain a satisfactory treatment of a façade which bends around a corner," they grumbled. They were classicists, of course, and thought in terms of symmetry, not of form following function, nor, as the layman Eastman did, of attracting the largest crowds, nor, as modernists such as I. M. Pei would, of fitting the building to its trapezoidal lot. Furthermore, they did not like the elliptical corner lobby with its low ceiling which appeared on the Eastman/Kaelber plans and felt that a 3,300-seat auditorium was much too large for Rochester. They foresaw crowds being throttled and disoriented as they entered and left the auditorium, particularly in the area behind the orchestra seats.

The delay in contacting the New York firm was calculated. "They are the best decorators in the country," Eastman once explained cavalierly, "but I wouldn't let them near the plans." Why? "A floor plan is an engineering proposition, and must take precedent over the architecture in any commercial scheme." Thus, as Eastman told Larry White, "It is a set policy in all my building operations to work out the plans myself with all its details before calling in an architect." White, who had inherited his father's facile sketching talents and interest in classical detail, had never heard of such a policy. The Eastman Theatre was to be his first major project, and he was anxious to salvage it if he could.

For his part, Eastman wanted White and his colleagues primarily to ensure that "a house of this size would not be 'barney' in character," as well as "to make the entrance foyer gay, bright, and beautiful," the second balcony "warm and rich in color, and beautiful in proportion and details…and in every respect just as attractive a place to sit and safe to walk in as the main floor," and to plan for "indirect lighting throughout so people can walk in without stumbling." It was not the kind of secondary decorative assignment the prestigious firm was accustomed to tackling. Indeed, they "felt justified in asking a substantial sum for our services. I do not believe anybody can criticize a professional fee of $15,000," Fenner confided. "If we can bring some architectural order out of the present chaotic plan, that service alone will be worth all that Mr. Eastman will pay for it." But Eastman decided $12,000 was what decorating skills were

Architect William Kaelber drew the plan to Eastman's instructions.

New York architect Lawrence Grant White, a classicist, thought the Eastman/Kaelber plan to be "an abomination" and walked off the job, only to return later.

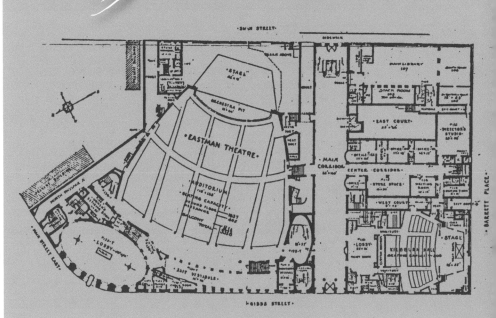

Brooklyn peacemaker Frank Babbott, who had engaged McKim, Mead & White in 1902 to work on Eastman's house, coaxed them to come back and finish decorating the exterior and interior of the Eastman Theatre and School of Music.

The Drama of the Skewed Axis

By 13 September 1921, the Eastman School of Music was finished and open for faculty and students, and a steel frame was up for the Eastman Theatre (left). Note the apartment house at left whose owner declined to sell, thereby skewing forever the axis of the Eastman Theatre.

worth. "The Eastman matter is a troublesome one," Fenner reported to Mead, somewhat later. "With the plan Kaelber has developed it will be exceedingly difficult to get adequate architectural treatment for the Court Auditorium and its approaches. We submitted an alternate plan…. Mr. Eastman was skeptical in the extreme and said he was unwilling to sacrifice anything whatever to architecture either as to seating capacity or service arrangements…. He said he would build a perfectly plain brick barn if he felt he could thereby bring music to the largest number."

As with the Kodak camera, the "largest" was also the magic number to Eastman. The New York architects, he felt, were engaging in elitist thinking: their view was "the old-fashioned one that the chief effort should be to please the occupants of the best seats," Eastman told his oldest and closest friend, Frank Babbott. "Of course, it is this class who support concerts and operas but they are not the ones I am after in my scheme." Worst of all, the McKim, Mead & White plan "used the very corner of the plot, which is one of the most important in the city, for service stairs and elevator…. We had a mighty nice interview but I suppose right down in their hearts Messrs. Kendall and White think I am a pretty headstrong proposition and I think they are letting their art interfere with utility."

"Like most laymen he regards architecture merely as applied decoration," Fenner complained to Mead. "He says that if we admit the possibility of his plan…we can design a satisfactory auditorium, chamber music hall, entrances, and a good exterior. All of which we admit we can do. He fails to see the point when we contend that still the building will be architecturally poor.

I tried to illustrate my point by telling him that occasionally the Lord made a hunchback, …and he might give the hunchback a beautiful head…but when he was through, he had still only a poor misshapen creature…. Dr. Rhees smiled and saw the point but Mr. Eastman did not admit the parallel…. Mr. Eastman flatly refused to consider any changes in the Music School and by his instructions confined us to restudy the big auditorium itself."

"He did make one important concession," Fenner wrote. Because Eastman was just leaving for a six-week trip to the Rocky Mountains, McKim, Mead & White were allowed that time to whip their proposition into order. Meanwhile, Fenner would go back to the man who originally introduced Eastman and William Mead, Frank Babbott. "I shall try to see Mr. Babbott and…ask him to advise. Kendall, Richardson, and I all feel that rather than accept the plan as it stands and the responsibility for it which would certainly be placed upon us by the public, we would withdraw from the work…."

The Elliptical Lobby

In the alloted time, mid-August to October, the New York architects prepared a plan which, they told Eastman, "equals yours but is structurally more direct and straightforward." Eastman did not agree that this was the best solution and would hear nothing about decreasing the number of seats or giving up "the spacious stairways and ramp from the mezzanine to the second balcony…." He conveyed his objections in a letter that ran for several pages.

"The exterior is built of limestone in a free adaption of the Italian Renaissance style," stated an article in the 3 February 1923 issue of The American Architect: The Architectural Review. *"The dignity of a public institution is emphasized rather than the gaiety of a theatre. An order of Ionic pilasters, broken at the two entrances by engaged columns of Vermont marble (by a curious coincidence, known to the trade as 'Eastman green'), serves to give unity to the main façade."*

Nov. 13, 1921

Eastman wrote:

> I could not help feeling when you left me yesterday afternoon that you did not realize what you were up against in endeavoring to change the floor plan.... It may be that 3,500 seating capacity is a little ahead of its time.... The seats are expected to yield $150 per annum. If the capacity is reduced only 200 the receipts would be reduced $30,000. Capitalized this would mean $600,000.... If it turns out we are unable to fill the house…rather than cut it out I would erect a semi-permanent curtain to cut off the upper third or half of the gallery. I cannot think that the…axis of the auditorium is a matter that will ever be noticed by the public.... I, myself, much prefer the elliptical lobby to the circular one.

ahead…but without much hope.... Eastman is such a big factor in Rochester that people do not argue with him but accept what he says as law. I doubt whether his own friends dare to advise him honestly when they think he has made a mistake and if we were to decline further association with his work, I think it would be a very great surprise to him and possibly make him reconsider.

Instead, it was the New York architects who were in for the surprise. Eastman impassively listened to their arguments, watched them walk off the job after Mead cabled Fenner to do so, had them return their drawings, then summoned William G. Kaelber and, at this crisis moment, immediately plunged into another enormous undertaking: the cutting in half of his

Eastman is such a big factor in Rochester that people do not argue with him but accept what he says as law. — Burt Fenner

Fenner reported to Mead:

> You may think we have gone too far in offering to do more work and then if he does not like it, offer to retire and waive all claims to reimbursement, but Mr. Eastman took the position…that there had been a perfectly distinct understanding…that we were to go ahead…unless we could devise a plan which contained every single detail of arrangement which his plan showed. He felt we had failed to do so.... They think our plan is impossible from an operating point of view.... Mr. Eastman's attitude was and still is perfectly courteous and friendly.... We are therefore going

four-story concrete and steel home in order to enlarge the conservatory by nine feet four inches.

He then turned to another matter that had long occupied his attention: the swift and orderly removal of every diseased tonsil in Rochester. Only after the successful completion of the Great Housecutting Caper and the Great Tonsilectomy Marathon did he return to his long-range projects of establishing a first-rate music school in Rochester.

Return of the Prodigal Architects

McKim, Mead & White, having reduced their fees "below what we think our services are worth," returned in 1920 at the urging of Frank Babbott to finish the limestone façade and interior decorations of the Eastman Theatre and School of Music.

The resumption of the project coincided with Eastman's return from his three-week visit to Japan. As a condition of their return, Eastman issued a directive that all publicity was to state that McKim, Mead & White were "not responsible for the plan."

The name of the complex was not yet settled, however. "What would you think," Eastman asked Rush Rhees in 1921, "of calling the school the Academy of Music and this [music] hall the Academy of Motion Pictures, that title to go on the frieze over the portico, the advertising name for motion picture purposes to be Academy Theater?" During construction, the hoarding exhibited these names. But Rhees and the university trustees saw advertising purposes better served by "Eastman Theatre." Once the donor, who had always maintained that the only thing he wanted to see his name on was the company he founded, was convinced of the financial soundness of their notion, he acquiesced. Building strikes delayed construction; the school opened its temporary doors to students in September 1921 amid the clatter of riveting and hammering. The theater was only a steel frame and classes were held on the third and fourth floors of the school, the only finished areas.

Architecturally, the Beaux-Arts trained Lawrence Grant White pleased everyone with his Palladian façade for the Eastman School so well, in fact, that when a poll of Rochester architects was taken in 1980, they picked the 1922 Eastman Theatre as the best building in town. But in the 1920s, a national magazine dismissed the effort cavalierly: "A $17 million school of music is…somewhat grandiose for a town of Rochester's size."

A Zodiac Problem

Larry White had fun with his own special "problem in architectural astronomy" and being a strict classicist like his father, worried about not getting it just right.

"On the ceiling is an annular band decoration in which the signs of the Zodiac occur in twelve circular panels," White wrote to Robert Burnside Potter, an astronomy expert. "I feel sure that some captious scientist will remark that they are not properly oriented as was the case in the ceiling of the waiting room of Grand Central Terminal. Assuming a person is lying on his back and looking up at the ceiling, on what compass bearings would Aries appear and should Taurus be to the right or left of it?"

"The dignity of a public institution is emphasized rather than the gaiety of a theatre," an article in *The American Architect* reported. The color of the engaged columns of Vermont marble flanking the entrances were, by a curious coincidence, known as "Eastman green." Topping the façade was the inscription, crafted by Rush Rhees to express Eastman's objective, FOR THE ENRICHMENT OF COMMUNITY LIFE.

Very little escaped Eastman's attention. Of A. A. Hopeman, general contractor, he inquired, "Would it not be well to have some extra tile laid on the flat roof so that they can weather in case they are needed for repairs. If we are to put in a few spic and span new tiles some day…it would ruin the beauty of the roof." And when a friend suggested that Eastman have his portrait painted for the lobby, Eastman had his own suggestion: "Would it not satisfy your portrait aspirations if I should be sculpt'd heroic size for one of the figures on the roof, with a camera in one hand and a horn in the other?"

Inside, the effect of the oval lobby, which the New York architects deplored but agreed to decorate, and the other public rooms to which they added their inimitable touches, was akin to the decor of an ocean liner. Twelve Psyche and Cupid panels celebrating that ancient Greek myth were printed in fifty shades of gray for the lobby and mezzanine. Based on drawings by Jacques Louis David, the woodblocks were commissioned by Napoleon and first cut and printed in 1814 by Louis Lafitte. Reprinted only once, in 1923, at the behest of classicist Lawrence Grant White, the blocks have since been dispersed. In 1972 these wallpaper scenes, blackened with age and beyond repair, were replaced by an identical set from the original woodblocks. The major change of the 1972 renovation was to remove the 10,000 pipes of the defunct organ for a modern air conditioning system.

Chandelier and Murals

From a gilded sunburst in the coffered, domed ceiling was hung one of the largest chandeliers in existence. Built in this country on site in 1922, the chandelier is outfitted in Czechoslovakian crystal. (For more about the chandelier, see page 110.)

"Interlude," a jewel-like painting by Maxfield Parrish, was purchased for the landing of the stairs leading to the loges, and Eastman declared it a "peacherina." Also in the mezzanine was a "beautiful allegorical painting of the Renaissance period formerly in a well known collection." Eastman bought it from Stanford White's estate through his son.

Eight murals were commissioned of Barry Faulkner and Ezra Winter for the side walls beginning at the level of the loges. Painted in the full flush of the romanticism of the period, Faulkner's murals on the right represent Religious, Hunting, Pastoral, and Dramatic Music while Winter's on the left represent Festival, Lyric, Martial, and Sylvan Music, all posed against Italian landscapes. Winter immortalized his friends, including architect Will Kaelber on horseback, as models for the paintings. The murals also occasioned a row between the Rochester and New York architects on a basic level: design versus acoustics. (For more about the murals, see pages 98-109.)

Maxfield Parrish was the most popular artist of the 1920s; so it is not surprising that Lawrence Grant White chose him to complete the theater's artistic input. When Parrish's painting arrived at the theater, Eastman looked it over and pronounced it a "peacherina." With Eastman, a peach was good but a peacherina was the best—he rated his five cars with those adjectives, too. Eastman, who had the only Old Master collection in Rochester, also thought the picture was "very strong, simple, forceful." There is a persistent rumor that Parrish used some young women of Rochester as models for the figures portrayed against that Parrish blue sky. Most mentioned are the beautiful daughters of Libanus Todd, brother of Eastman's friend George W. Todd. Those who subscribe to this view will tell you that even in her eighties, Peggy Todd Kearns (who started the rumor) had the same profile as the young woman in the middle. The Libanus Todd family played host to Ezra Winter, too, during the years, ça. 1920–1927, that he was working on Rochester buildings and doing his preliminary sketching at the Todd home on Lake Ontario. "Interlude" hung at one end of the grand balcony foyer for seven decades, deteriorating from the temperature changes of an outside wall and the touch of grubby fingerprints of those coming up the stairs, before it was removed to the University of Rochester's Memorial Art Gallery and replaced by a life-sized photograph of itself.

"Interlude" by Maxfield Parrish

"Mrs. Harold" and Peacock Alley

At his request "Mrs. Harold" (Marian Gleason) accompanied him shipboard from Paris to New York after one of his African trips.

Shortly after the opening of the Eastman Theatre, a new magazine, *fiveO'clock*, featured George Eastman on its cover. The ubiquitous newspaperman Henry Clune was its managing editor and chief reporter, covering the parade of fashionably dressed social leaders who promenaded through the mezzanine, causing him to hail it as

Marian Gleason

Maria Kilbourn Eastman

"Rochester's Peacock Alley." "Mrs. Harold" (Marian Gleason) was an Eastman favorite, part of the "Lobster Quartet" of four young women who came to lunch each Saturday at Eastman's home and usually dined on lobster with their host. It was said that she reminded him of his mother and, indeed, there is a resemblance between her photograph and an 1850 daguerreotype of the young Maria Kilbourn Eastman.

DESIGN VERSUS ACOUSTICS

In his new design, White wanted to raise the theater ceiling and standardize the coffers. "Unless it will really be a great improvement," Will Kaelber wrote, "we…are informed by Dr. [Floyd R.] Watson, the acoustical expert [from Urbana, Illinois], that this is the ideal ceiling height from the standpoint of acoustics…. Also, the more the coffers are varied in pattern the better…. We do not wish to appear to be dictating…merely passing along suggestions," Kaelber continued. Next came an argument over how many square feet of sound absorbent surface in the form of quilted felt panels were needed. "I cannot agree," Kaelber wrote, "that it is well to defer the felt panels until such time as the need is demonstrated. Should we wait and the hall be bad, nothing that we could do to change the conditions would ever catch up with the story of our failure to produce a good room from an acoustical standpoint. The auditorium must be correct acoustically, or as near as possible, the first night that it is used by the public."

To create the illusion of a massive stone-walled Medici palace but still have thermal insulation properties for an outside wall, White ordered a composition board called Zenitherm. ("Looks like stone, works like wood; waterproof, inert and durable; installed by carpenters not masons," read the ads—see page 94.) Those interior walls of Zenitherm are so eye-fooling that the skeptic must touch to confirm that the coldness of real stone is absent.

The acoustics versus design conflict raged for some time. White was appalled at suggestions by his own acoustical experts that gilt-tinted felt be applied to the ceiling, and even more aghast at the idea of placing the Faulkner and Winter paintings on

Acoustical experts recommend that the more the coffers are varied in size the better.

stretchers with springs to prevent buckling and felt behind them: "Absolutely impractical!" he thundered. "For best results, paintings should be made in place on a plaster wall as with the great Italian mural paintings. Next best is to mount the canvas on the wall…but the slightest wrinkle will absolutely detract from the effectiveness of mural painting…." As an alternative White suggested "panels of felt covered with velvet hangings which can be removed if not needed."

The Eastman Theatre, up until 2009 one of the largest concert halls in the country, was initially pronounced as acoustically one of the best. The Polish pianist Ignace Jan Paderewski, who played on 15 November 1922 at one of the opening concerts, called it "the finest temple of music" in which he had ever tickled the ivories. More recent conductors of the Rochester Philharmonic Orchestra such as David Zinman and Mark Elder have deemed it less than perfect. Its original dual function as both movie theater and concert hall meant that compromises had to be made which affected it in both roles.

The Subscribers Entrance remains the carriage entrance to the mezzanine, the "Diamond Horseshoe" of the Eastman Theatre. A beautiful elliptical stair rises to a richly furnished lobby. Construction delays meant that this entrance was not used until several weeks after the theater opened.

Eastman was no sentimentalist, but that emotion triumphed fifty years later when the Eastman Kodak Company undertook to restore the faded elegance of Mr. Eastman's theater.

Washtub Chandeliers

A day before the theater opened, a tour of inspection convinced Eastman that the two rear corners of the balcony were not adequately lighted by the enormous chandelier that hung from the center of the ceiling. All electrical fixtures had been designed and specially constructed by E. F. Caldwell & Company, premier producers of electroliers in the country. Obviously there was no time to get a Caldwell fixture, yet "can't" was not a word in Eastman's vocabulary. Within hours, ingenious artisans were rigging up two ordinary corrugated metal washtubs with chains for hanging. For decoration they used a two-inch rope

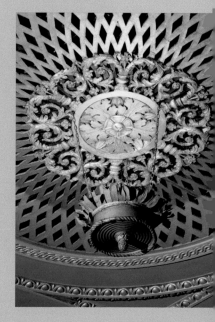

along the bottom rim. From a nearby florist came a wreath of immortelles which was draped from the upper rim, while a plaster pineapple, left over from the theater ceiling, was fixed to the center of each tub bottom. Gilded and wired, the tubs were installed as a temporary solution. Amused by their incongruity but amazed at their effectiveness, Eastman decided not to replace them. The washtubs are still there, lighting the dark corners of the second balcony.

Labor Day 1922 is Opening Day of the movies: Flags flew over the longest marquee in the world (right).

What Shall We Name It?

As the theater was under construction, the hoarding announced that it would be called the National Academy of Motion Pictures. What would the Oscar home have been called if that name had stuck?

On 10 September 1922, the *Democrat & Chronicle* jumped the gun and drew the letters "Eastman Theater" on a photo of the façade (below right). But the Francophile architect Larry White, who had lived for years in Paris, had another spelling in mind. By opening day, stone masons had carved the French version of the word and the theater became officially and forever the Eastman Theatre.

Public sentiment demanded keeping the golden washtubs (see anecdote page 37), and they did. Also at that grand reopening of 7 January 1972, every seat was occupied but one. In another bow to sentiment, Eastman's chair—Number 48 in first row of the mezzanine along the right aisle—had been recovered but not renumbered.

George W. Todd accompanied Eastman during his eleventh-hour inspection tour on Labor Day Eve 1922, and there was a lot of shifting around of furniture to achieve the effect most sought. When the lobby seemed satisfactory, there was one console table left over. Eastman looked around, spotted a mirror or two on the sidewalls and decided to place the table under one of them, remarking that it would make a handy place for women to lay their purses while looking in the mirror to adjust their hats or apply lipstick. "It takes a bachelor to know all about women," Todd was heard to murmur.

In all, some 2,500 blueprints were drafted and between 500 and 700 workmen employed to create the Eastman School and Theatre. This phase brought its creator more pleasure than the massive public acclaim that followed in its wake. The process rather than the product was the exciting part: "The fun is in the game more than listening to the mostly unintelligent holler about it," Eastman wrote his cousin in Waterville.

As a labor of fun as well as art, the elegant theater has aged gracefully, remaining one of the magnificent concert halls of the nation. A poll of architects in the mid 1980s named it Rochester's most beautiful and architecturally significant building—despite the presence of works by Frank Lloyd Wright and I. M. Pei—and despite the continuing fact that post-concert crowds still bottleneck when trying to leave via Mr. Eastman's elliptical lobby. The 2004-2010 renovation and expansion corrected some acoustical deficits while enhancing the elegance and adding to the utility.

For the enrichment of
community life. —Rush Rhees

There seems to be a natural alliance between music and pictures. —George Eastman

The Eastman Theatre, a financial as well as artistic marriage of his two loves, music and film, was pure George Eastman.

Flags of many nations streamed above the marquee when the Eastman Theatre opened its doors for the glittering "Dress Performance" on the evening of 2 September 1922. Car after car glided to the entrance for that first 9 o'clock evening performance. Splendid dignitaries emerged and promenaded into the theater in full evening dress. A dozen limousines remained parked across Gibbs Street for the duration of the presentation; chauffeurs chatted softly together and smoked until the carriage call indicated their charges had issued forth. George Eastman arrived with his guests, Rush and Harriet Rhees. Expressionless, he stood rigidly still for a moment, then acknowledged the applauding crowd with a deep bow and headed straight for his four reserved seats, front row right, 42 to 48 (the last his own) in the mezzanine, which he always paid for whether he occupied them or not. The inconspicuous (to the rest of the audience) mezzanine could accommodate numerous private parties, sandwiched as it was between the

"As I am very much interested in music as well as in pictures, I am going to build in Rochester a motion picture house with the view of using music and pictures in alliance."

—George Eastman

vast main floor with its rich if chilly grandeur and the equally capacious balcony. The mezzanine promenade quickly became Rochester's "Peacock Alley." As many people came to see the most palatial theater in America and the parade of fashionably dressed social leaders as came to see the movies or hear the music.

Eastman, the entrepreneur of music for the masses, wanted every seat in the house to be a good one. Since the auditorium was curved rather than a simple rectangle, the floor had to be concave so that seats on the same row would be at the same elevation. Consequently the theater had one of the first "dished floors" ever built. Ironically, because the exclusive mezzanine was tucked under the balcony for

Victor Wagner conducting a WHAM orchestra in the late 1920s

the privacy of the elite, the well-heeled suffered the worst acoustics in the house.

Two days later, on Labor Day 4 September, the public streamed in for the official opening. "Performances De Luxe" of motion pictures accompanied by carefully selected orchestral or

The mezzanine was "Peacock Alley."

George Eastman's chair endures.

THIS CHAIR WAS OCCUPIED BY MR. EASTMAN FROM 1921 WHEN THIS THEATRE WAS OPENED UNTIL HIS DEATH IN 1932.

The Prisoner of Zenda was the opening film on 4 September 1922.

organ music were scheduled for 2:15, 7, and 9 p.m. Each "programme" opened with Arthur Alexander or his assistant, Victor Wagner, conducting an orchestra of fifty members decked out in the uniforms of a marching band. This was followed by "Eastman Theatre Current Events," a one-reel film produced by Fox Films which showed various aspects of the new building, and then by "Music Interpreted Through the Dance." In this last, dancer Esther Gustafson interpreted "Russia" through Rachmaninoff's *G Minor Prelude*, and "The South at Work" through Dvořák's *Humoresque in A Minor*. Next came an "Eastman Theatre Magazine" of short subjects compiled by Charles Goulding, the theater's first manager, which included color footage produced by John Capstaff's early Eastman Kodachrome process of 1914 and projected "for the first time on any screen." The program for that first week had distinctly Russian overtones, beginning with Tchaikovsky's *1812 Overture*. The feature film was Rex Ingram's production of *The Prisoner of Zenda*—"precisely as now shown at $1.50 prices at Astor Theatre, New York." A spine-tingling *Organ Exit* with Dezso d'Antalffy or John Hammond on the great Austin theater organ completed the show.

A month later the theater hosted its first opera, a whole week of *Aida* by Verdi, produced by the San Carlo Opera Company. Eastman's "nice houseful of guests" and Rochester's large Italian community gave the company the greatest reception in its history—nearly full houses for eight performances. "The way the Italian people turned out was remarkable even for such a music loving nation," Eastman told the consul. The Boston and New York Symphonies came in November along with the first solo recital by pianist Ignace Jan Paderewski. The famous names in the music world—Ballet Russes, the Ukrainian Chorus, the London String Quartet, the Cleveland Orchestra—soon made Rochester a regular stop.

Eastman's musical egalitarianism showed in the sale of tickets, which was on a first-come basis in order to avoid any "class distinctions." Admission for afternoon shows ranged from twenty cents for the grand balcony to fifty cents for the mezzanine, and evening prices ranged from thirty-five cents to a dollar. One section of the mezzanine, however, was reserved for the 600 Subscribers Association patrons who contributed at least $150 a year.

In its own time, the Eastman Theatre was as remarkable as the Radio City Music Hall would be later. In the early 1920s, there were few theaters in the country to compare with it. Four that did were the Rialto, the Rivoli, the Capital (seating 5,000) and the Roxy Theatres in New York City—all the achievements of a great showman, Samuel L. "Roxy" Rothapfel. Roxy was initially slated to run the Eastman Theatre. But Roxy did not get the job, and the earnest but eventually ineffective Charles Goulding was chosen. When he did not work out, William Fait Jr came and went, as did Eric Thacher Clarke, son of Eastman's old patent expert and colleague.

Under Eastman's 1919 contract with the University of Rochester, he had transferred the site (for which he paid about $381,000) and the funds "necessary to erect

Paderewski and Eastman were acquainted even before the Eastman Theatre was built.

CABLE ADDRESS "HAM NEW YORK"   TELEPHONE 2200 CIRCLE.

HOTEL GOTHAM

FIFTH AVENUE AT FIFTY-FIFTH STREET

NEW YORK

WETHERBEE & WOOD. PROPR'S.   February 28th, 1921.

Mr. George Eastman,
c/o Eastman Kodak Company,
Rochester, New York.

Dear Mr. Eatman,

    Mr. Falerski delivered to me in Pittsburgh your cordial letter of February 22nd.

    Both my wife and myself, vividly remember the courtesy which you so kindly extended to us on our last visit to Rochester and I can assure you that your present invitation to your own house is more than tempting to us. Please receive our sincere thanks for your gracious offer of hospitality which we would be honored and pleased to accept, were it not for our present inability to go to Rochester, due to numerous previous engagements and the necessity of our leaving for California on March 15th, at the very latest.

    In a letter to the Rochester Chamber of Commerce I am asking its distinguished members to favor me by postponing their invitation until my return from the West, which will take place sometime toward the middle of May.

    Hoping that they will not refuse me my request, I am looking forward, dear Mr. Eastman, with a great deal of anticipated pleasure, to seeing you again, at that time.

    With renewed thanks and very best regards, in which my wife joins me, I remain

        Sincerely yours,

        J. J. Paderewski

Eastman or his secretary, Alice K. Whitney (right), was empowered to draw from the building fund, with the treasurer of the university next in line "in the event of my death."

and equip and endow said buildings" while at the same time "controlling the expenditure of such money…with like authority and effect as though he retained the ownership and possession of the money necessary for such purposes." The music school was to be run by a separate board of directors nominated by Eastman and approved by the university board of trustees. A building fund account was set up into which he would "from time to time deposit sufficient sums with which to erect…a large concert and motion picture hall,…a smaller concert or recital hall, and a power plant…in accordance with plans and specifications prepared under and in accordance with his own directions." Eastman or his secretary, Alice K. Whitney, was empowered to draw from this fund, with the treasurer of the university next in line "in the event of my death." The endowment was to be kept in "good securities" and the two halls were to "be used for motion picture exhibitions or entertainments as well as musical, social, educational, convention, religious or public assemblage purposes with or without charge of admission under rules prescribed by the board of directors…. All proceeds derived from motion picture and other entertainments…carried on in the large hall shall be used for purposes of maintaining an orchestra for said hall and the furtherance of musical interests in Rochester." The university was to insure all this and it was allowed, at some future date, to move the school to the campus of the university or anywhere else as long as similar buildings and equipment were provided. Eastman's final clause stipulated that "none of the income from endowment may be used for the maintenance of the orchestra as he does not intend to endow the orchestra, nor does he desire to contribute to its maintenance beyond any such proceeds as may be available from the operation of the large concert and motion picture hall." Eastman's philosophy was to endow music education, which was basic, but not an orchestra, which would spring up naturally if people were sufficiently educated. Beneath the bold and rolling signature "George Eastman," is the much smaller scratch of the co-signer, Rush Rhees.

The Movies

When Rush Rhees first learned of Eastman's plan to build a motion picture theater as part of the music school, the news "nearly gave me apoplexy," Rhees admitted later. He recovered when he learned that Eastman planned to endow the complex.

Rhees's initial shock when he realized that he, a university president and Baptist minister, would be running a silent movie house was a residual effect of the movies' initial reputation as a purveyor of frivolous and morally suspect entertainment for lowlifes. By 1919, however, movies were no longer "flickers"—they now featured Roman legions and mighty sea battles in many reels, and spiritually uplifting messages as well. Instead of a mechanical piano to accompany them, the services of an organ or orchestra were enlisted. Movies were now respectable and popular with all social classes. The auditoriums where they were shown underwent a similar epic transformation. Seeking to outdo the splendors of the rented opera houses, movie impresarios built palaces of marble and decorated them with all that was ornate in chandeliers and other fixtures. Eastman always thought movies

Peter Pan *(below) was one of the early silent movies shown in the theater.*

were respectable—they used a great supply of film.

At the Eastman Theatre, movies in total darkness were eliminated by a special lighting system developed by the Kodak Research Laboratories "which makes it possible to supply sufficient light in all parts of the theatre for patrons to find seats without halting or groping, see all the objects in the auditorium and read the printed programme.... This improvement removes the discomfort, inconvenience and moral hazard inescapable when audiences are assembled in darkened auditoriums and, it is hoped, will overcome existing prejudice of parents... against motion picture entertainment." Some were intimidated by Eastman's enforced rules of decorum. "Real movie fans were awed by the aseptic and cavernous bulk of the theatre," wrote Roger Butterfield, who worked on a biography of Eastman that was never published. "They didn't like the half-lighting that continued through all performances." Instead, they were "used to dank, pitch-dark places where you could drop peanut shells and stick gum on the seats. The place was just too imposing."

The Movies Are Back!

In December 2008 the Rochester Philharmonic Orchestra performed the sound track to the British holiday classic *The Snowman* as part of the orKIDstra Holiday Special. Some 2500 children of all ages filled the theater

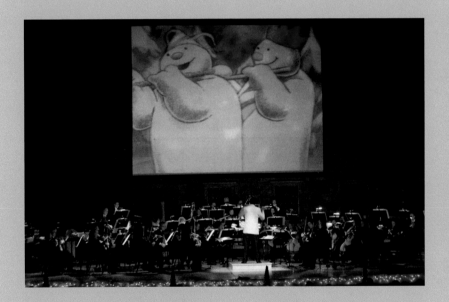

that day, making it the most successful orKIDstra concert to that date. It was one of the first movies shown with live music in Eastman Theatre since the 1920s and showcased one of the original functions of the Eastman Theatre, which was to combine live orchestral music with the movies.

The movie The Snowman *is based on the book by Raymond Briggs with the music composed by Howard Blake.*

A New Career

With the school and theater Eastman was starting a new career, running it as closely as he used to run the Eastman Kodak Company. He made notes commenting on theater advertising layouts, the size of lettering on screen announcements, or drawings for cartoons. He answered petty complaints from movie goers. His daily inspections were so punctual and punctilious that the nervous staff and students could set their watches by his arrival each morning on his way to work.

He stayed close always to the theater/school exchequer. On the dot of nine he appeared in the office of Arthur See, secretary-manager of the Eastman School with the usual query, "What's the worst you know?" See had already positioned the daily financial report on the lower right-hand corner of the blotter on his desk. See did not like Eastman, and Eastman was wary of See, especially after the latter moved on to become secretary of the Civic Music Association in 1930 and began manipulating his contracts with both the school and CMA in such a way that his salary was doubled. Eastman immediately spotted this and dropped See from the school's payroll. Yet See outlasted all the theater managers, to say nothing of school director Klingenberg and orchestra director Alexander, both of whom Eastman fired. He was still secretary of the CMA when he died in his sleep in 1953.

Following Eastman's ingrained pattern of inspecting and manipulating everything at home and at work, during the construction period Eastman scrutinized the theater and music school for the possibility of nail holes that needed filling and studied carefully the height of the coat racks. A door one-quarter-inch off plumb could provoke the fulmination, "What wood butcher did that?" Once the school was in operation, Eastman was known to startle the occupant of a studio by striding in to put the furniture back where he believed it should belong.

At five in the afternoon, on his way home from work, Eastman stopped by the theater to examine the day's attendance receipts. Many afternoons he stopped first at the drugstore across East Main from the theater. While chauffeur Harvey Padelford waited discreetly at the curb in the green Cunningham, the Kodak mogul, still in his white lab coat, would mount a high stool amongst the other kids and order a ten-cent malted which came with a free cookie (two free cookies when Mr. Eastman was present). Frequently, as when his latest hunting trophies were on view in the upstairs corridor between theater and school, he conducted informal tours for the drugstore kids and other Eastman Preparatory School students. More at ease with children than adults, he remembered their names and bantered lightly with them. A more informal atmosphere prevailed on those afternoons than at the Sunday night concerts at Eastman's home where the same kids, in best bib and tucker, were admonished sternly not to pick the oranges from the giant tree in the conservatory.

Late at night Eastman would steal into the theater to preview new movies. During the day the Kodak staff had been drawing up charts and doing statistical studies measuring the audience appeal of various films. When Rush Rhees received letters of complaint about Greta Garbo and John Gilbert's eroticism in Clarence Brown's 1927 silent *The Flesh and the Devil*, Eastman examined it and reported that "of course all of these so-called sex pictures are objectionable but I saw nothing unusually so, or that could be cut out except perhaps the unusually prolonged kissing." He told Rhees's secretary Carl Lauterbach, "If the theatre is compelled to cut out everything that could be put in this class it would have to close its doors."

Starring Greta Garbo...

Greta Garbo starred in the silent flickers that George Eastman previewed on his late night visits to his theater.

James Card, a devotee of Garbo, was considered the greatest authority in the country on early motion pictures and owner of one of the three great film collections in the world. In 1972, on the fiftieth anniversary of the Eastman Theatre, Card wrote: "Mr. Eastman determined to build a film theatre to outshine them all. His love for music and his appreciation of the film medium he had done so much to advance were not separable qualities. Mr. Eastman was a man no more given to hyperbole than was Calvin Coolidge. Yet in 1919, he revealed his faith in cinema in these words:

'Today is the day of revelation for the motion picture. Today it is being realized more and more that the screen is a better medium for the transmission of ideals and thoughts than the printed book. One can easily forget what one reads in a book . . . But this is not so with the Picture play which, by appealing to the eye with artistic photography and the soul with music in the symphony or organ, drives home inescapably great truths and ideas to an audience. I look forward to the wide-spread presentation soon of motion pictures in our largest theatres.'"

Through Klingenberg, Eastman negotiated for over a year with Finnish composer Jan Sibelius to teach fugue and composition at the school, and in January 1921, press notices appeared that Sibelius had been engaged. Telegrams and editorials praised "the selection as an augury of the standard which will prevail in your admirable institution." In August 1920 Klingenberg had gone to Stockholm, cabling back that Sibelius wanted $20,000 for the academic year. Eastman agreed and assumed the matter settled, but later Sibelius begged off, pleading ill health. Anxious to recruit an internationally famous composer, Eastman and company considered Sergei Rachmaninoff. Finally Klingenberg arranged for Christian Sinding—talented pianist, composer, and personal friend—to come to Rochester, where he taught theory and composition for two years, his only venture outside Norway. Sinding is best remembered for one of music's great chestnuts, *Rustle of Spring,* which brought his name into many a genteel parlor in Europe and the Americas. Upon arriving in Rochester, Sinding composed a work for organ dedicated to Eastman. "As Mr. Sinding does not speak English, he has tried to express his feelings in this piece of music 'Hymnus' for the organ," his wife Augusta Sinding wrote to Eastman, "composed to tell you how he appreciates all you have done for the music and all you are going to do for the music. He is trying to thank you in this way."

Selim Palmgren, Finnish composer, pianist, and conductor, arrived from Helsinki in 1923 as a teacher of composition. His were mostly choral or orchestral works in Swedish or Finnish, or small-scale piano pieces incorporating Finnish folk rhythms. Clearly, the gentle Klingenberg's Scandinavian contacts made an impact in forming the early faculty, and Palmgren occasionally played at Eastman's home for the Sunday musicales.

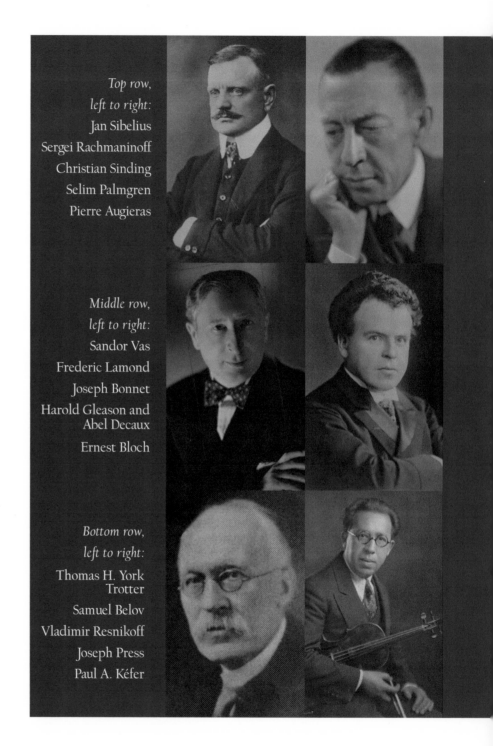

Top row, left to right:
Jan Sibelius
Sergei Rachmaninoff
Christian Sinding
Selim Palmgren
Pierre Augieras

Middle row, left to right:
Sandor Vas
Frederic Lamond
Joseph Bonnet
Harold Gleason and Abel Decaux
Ernest Bloch

Bottom row, left to right:
Thomas H. York Trotter
Samuel Belov
Vladimir Resnikoff
Joseph Press
Paul A. Kéfer

During those first two years of the Eastman School, the portals were open wide to many an international artist. Pierre Augieras, French pianist, gave lessons at the school. Sandor Vas from Hungary and Frederic Lamond from Scotland taught piano. Joseph Bonnet from France, foremost organist of the time, was succeeded by his countryman Abel Decaux. Swiss-born Ernest Bloch taught theory before returning to Cleveland. Thomas H. York Trotter from the Royal Academy used rhythm in his children's classes. Members of the Kilbourn Quartet, all first chairs in the Rochester Philharmonic Orchestra who also taught in the school, were the Russian Samuel Belov, the Czech Vladimir Resnikoff, the Hungarian Arthur Hartmann, and the Paris-educated Gustave Tinlot. Joseph Press, the leading cellist of the time, had to be met at the boat by interpreters assembled by Kodak in New York City. Gerald Maas and Paul A. Kéfer both trained abroad. Briton Thomas Austin-Bell and Russian Nicholas Konraty taught voice—and, unlike the majority of the above, both stayed for twenty years. Arthur Alexander, singer and conductor, himself was a New Zealander; the globe-trotting Albert Coates was Anglo-Russian by birth, and conductor Eugene Goossens hailed from Great Britain. And then there were legacies from the DKG Institute of Musical Art— the Norwegian-born Klingenberg, and Americans George B. Penny, Lucy Call, Mildred Brownell Mehlenbacher, and Arthur See.

Eastman's great vision of "building musical capacity on a large scale from childhood" led to the school being established not only as a collegiate institution within a university, but also as a music school for children and adults from the Rochester community. From 1921 on there has been a Preparatory Department (the present Eastman Community Music School) which offered not-for-credit, non-collegiate instruction to the community at large.

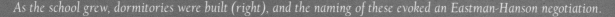

The school moved quickly toward professional status after the coming of Howard Hanson (below). Hanson was the son of Swedish immigrants, and many of his early compositions reflect his Scandinavian heritage.

As the school grew, dormitories were built (right), and the naming of these evoked an Eastman-Hanson negotiation.

A New Director and Program

The door to the Eastman School was often a revolving one. By 1923 Eastman had decided that Alf Klingenberg was not the person to get the school on track. "He had many admirable qualities," Eastman told conductor Albert Coates, "but he was not big enough to swing the job. What we want is a young man and our trustees think that he must be an American or an Englishman." One important problem had been, as Eastman noted, "Klingenberg did not like the theatre part" of Eastman's "scheme." And so the pianist's five-year contract as director was not renewed. This was a crushing blow to the Klingenbergs who, as Mrs. Klingenberg's letters to Eastman from Europe each summer attest, quite naturally looked on the happenings of the previous five years as a great chance. The Klingenbergs returned to Europe permanently that same year. "How many illusions we did have—and how hard to lose them all," Mrs. Klingenberg recalled years later.

The school moved quickly toward professional status after the coming of Howard Hanson. It more than doubled its original enrollment, and two annexes were built. A studio building, five stories high and available in 1924, housed the new opera department and was used for operatic and orchestral rehearsals and ballet training. The school became noted more for producing first-rate teachers and orchestra members than world-renowned virtuosos. Currently more than one-third of the administrators of outstanding American musical organizations are Eastman alumni.

As the school grew, dormitories were built, and the naming of these evoked an Eastman-Hanson negotiation. Eastman wanted to honor dead musicians from the classical past; Hanson, char-

The conservatory at Eastman's home (below) was where breakfast was served to architects and contractors who arrived overnight via the Empire State Limited train.

acteristically, wanted the dorms named for American composers. In a compromise, the names of three dead Americans—Francis A. Hopkinson, Edward B. MacDowell, and Stephen C. Foster—were inscribed on the new buildings. It took the students about five minutes to note that the middle initials of these notable composers were A, B, and C—and henceforth the three dorms would be known more by their initials than their names.

"Dear Rush," Eastman wrote the university president (after a quarter-century of friendship, the two men were on a first-name basis), "I withdraw my objections to American names for the dormitories. As long as the composers are dead and their historical background is satisfactory to the wise ones I am quite satisfied."

If he did not invent the breakfast meeting, Eastman certainly used it extensively. Wednesday night dinners might be social occasions with orchids and small talk, but the ritual breakfasts of construction days were for business. Lawrence Grant White regularly took the night train from New York. Breakfast was set "in a room so large that we needed an electric light over the table," White marveled. "As I was putting some excellent pancakes into my mouth, an organist—hidden behind a bank of a thousand cinerarias—played *The Maiden's Prayer* on an organ with the vox humana pulled out. The pancakes stuck in my throat."

Because Eastman was a trustee of the Metropolitan Opera, the company sometimes performed at his house. Here, the conservatory is set up for a production of Wolf-Ferrari's 1909 opera The Secret of Suzanne.

Vladimir Rosing

An opera buff since the 1890s and a member of the board of directors of the Metropolitan Opera since November 1920, Eastman had been cogitating about how to bring opera to Rochester when, on a transatlantic liner, he met "a somewhat eccentric, ostentatiously mannerist Russian tenor named Vladimir Rosing," as opera coach Nicolas Slonimsky would describe him, and unlikely as it seems, the American Opera Company was born. "American" meant that all operas were sung in English: Eastman favored opera in English because he considered it foolish to tell a long and complicated story that people couldn't understand.

Vladimir Rosing

From the start it was to be an experimental department at the school, financed for two years from its premiere performance in November 1924, although Rosing had been on Eastman's payroll since the summer of 1923. Eastman saw an opera class at the school as a way of getting "good singing acts" for the theater, because, as he told Roxy, "we are too far away from the supply of professional talent to do it in the way you are doing it so successfully." His goal for the 1923-1924 season was "to earn enough to finance the opera class…. With all of our mistakes we are going to get through the year with a whole skin, and a little to the good over." When the opera program was announced, it met with great approval from the Juilliard Foundation and the American Academy of Teachers of Singing as filling a void.

As the department developed, most of the instructors were Russian expatriates fleeing from the revolution. Russians were very much in fashion just then in the art and music worlds, and Rosing had received rave reviews in London from the likes of George Bernard Shaw and Ezra Pound and as a result had landed a contract for a Canadian tour. He sang his Russian songs in a highly dramatic manner—drawing in his cheeks when performing Mussorgsky's *Songs of Death*, scratching himself all over for *Song of the Flea*, or dropping his jaw to portray the "village idiot."

In February 1927 at one of the last performances of the American Opera Company in Rochester, Mary Garden appeared in the title role of *Carmen*. Eastman and Garden's mother and sister, who came for the performance, sat in his usual seats. "One of the most convivial evenings I ever spent at his home was on

Opera star Mary Garden performed at the Eastman Theatre in 1927. At a party in her honor, newspaper writer and raconteur Henry Clune reported that George Eastman stared long and hard at Garden's strapless gown and finally wondered what was holding it up. "Only your age, Mr. Eastman," came the reply from Garden.

Rouben Mamoulian was featured in a 1923 edition of The Note Book, *a periodical of the Eastman School of Music.*

ℛouben Mamoulian

Rosing immediately began recruiting his improbable staff from among the hundreds of emigré Russian musicians then in London and Paris. George W. Todd, music critic Jack Warner, and Rosing had alerted Eastman about a new play in London, the director of which was twenty-three-year-old Rouben Mamoulian, born in the Caucasus Mountains of Georgia of Armenian parents, a graduate of Moscow University in criminal law who had spent his evenings at the Moscow Art Theatre studying acting, writing, and directing. Tall, dark, and bespectacled, Mamoulian had produced *Rigoletto*, *Faust*, *Tannhäuser*, and Gilbert and Sullivan operettas in Moscow and would go on, after he left Rochester, to direct the first stage production of *Porgy and Bess* in 1935, to say nothing of a number of film classics, including *Dr. Jekyll and Mr. Hyde*, *Queen Christina*, and *Becky Sharp*, as well as many musicals. Mamoulian received a lengthy Eastman telegram recruiting him to help organize and direct the opera company and to teach "dramatic action." Mamoulian had just accepted a job at the Théatre des Champs-Elysées in Paris but decided to accept the unknown American millionaire's offer and asked to be let out of the Paris commitment. "You baffle me," said his Parisian employer. "Here I'm giving you a chance to be a director in the best theatre of the best city in the whole world, and you tell me you want to go to the country of barbarians, to the jungle? You will not be able to live there. They have no art. They are savages. You will be back."

For the first year or so, Mamoulian did not care for Eastman at all. He was just your typical idiosyncratic millionaire, Mamoulian decided, immensely intelligent but cold, monosyllabic, who wore this little black skull cap and looked like Pius XI—with whom Mamoulian had just had an audience.

the occasion of Mary Garden's visit…to sing in *Carmen* at one of our student performances," Eugene Goossens recalled. "His admiration for her was very obvious, and her approach to him was so refreshingly unconventional that he reacted instantaneously. Rarely did I see him in more jovial spirits nor so young in years as at that supper." Rosing's contract called for a New York performance of the opera company. In March 1927 Rochester's American Opera Company appeared for a week with the Theatre Guild in New York City with Eastman agreeing to "cover twenty-nine singers to perform *Seraglio*, *Figaro*, and *Madame Butterfly*." Conductor Eugene Goossens, nine men from the Eastman Theatre Orchestra, four of the stage crew, manager Arthur See, and several assistants were loaned to Rosing for the week. Critical acclaim for the New York performances led to new funding as the American Opera Company moved on to Chicago in 1928. "Mr. Rosing needs hard headed business control as much as money," Eastman warned the new supporters. But the Great Depression plus what Slonimsky calls "Rosing's miserable failure as an administrator" led to the company's disbanding in 1930.

During the two and a half years he spent in Rochester, Mamoulian directed the American Opera Company in about a dozen major productions. He was not enamored of opera in English: "We had to use those horrid translations." It was then, he said later, that he began to work towards "a truly dramatic theatre, a theatre that would combine all the elements of movement, dancing, acting, music, singing, decor, lighting, color, and so on." When Eastman asked him to take charge of all the musical presentations in the theater, Mamoulian agreed because he wanted to cook up a half-hour story with dialogue, dancing and singing—"I had that bee in my bonnet before I ever did *Porgy and Bess* or *Oklahoma!* or *Carousel*." But then Eastman tried to tell Mamoulian how it should be done and the two got into a terrible row. "Would I tell you how to run Kodak?" shouted Mamoulian. "You don't know what you're talking about," shouted Eastman, eyes ablaze, slamming his fist on the desk. Everybody in the school and theater ran for cover except Mamoulian, who just kept yelling. And then he looked at Eastman's eyes and realized that here was a verbal pugilist having his first real fight in forty years and relishing it thoroughly. When the argument was spent, Eastman stalked out but within the hour a messenger was back with an autographed photograph of Eastman. Mamoulian made his peace, too, in a 1925 letter to Eastman:

> ...everything has progressed splendidly.... I saw today the proofs of our short catalogue [of the new Eastman School of the Dance and Dramatic Action which Mamoulian started] which I had the pleasure of reading to you here some days ago. I have made out a budget....
>
> I want to thank you very much again for the time you gave to the consideration of affairs of our new school. I shall always remember the long conference with you, by which I must say I have greatly benefited. After it I feel even more enthusiastic

EASTMAN SCHOOL
OF THE
DANCE AND DRAMATIC ACTION
ROCHESTER, NEW YORK

29th July 1925

My dear Mr. Eastman,

This is only a proof of the letter-heads for our new School, the actual paper & print will be better, but I hope you like the style. I thought that this first proof could have no better addressie than the one whose name heads the title.

I want to thank you very much again for the time you gave to the consideration of affairs of our new school. I shall always remember the long conference with you, by which I must say I have greatly benefited. After it I feel even more enthusiastic and energetic than before.

Wishing you the best vacation I remain with my deep respect,
Yours very sincerely
Rouben Mamoulian

and energetic than before. I hope that you will allow me in the future to report some times to you personally about the progress of the school. Wishing you the best vacation I remain with my deep respect...

After that Mamoulian found Eastman fascinating—"and there are very few fascinating people in the world"—because he was mysterious. "There were dimensions in him that you would never suspect. You had to really penetrate and contact the deeper essence of the man. I loved him. A wonderful man. A highly honorable man which is more than you can say about a lot of rich men."

When Mamoulian reached what he considered "the end of my street" in Rochester, he told Eastman he was going to New York. "New York is tough," Eastman counseled, not unsympathetically since he gave Mamoulian two months to try it out with a guaranteed job if he returned. Mamoulian went and returned: "Nobody wants me," he said. So Eastman gave him letters of introduction to Broadway moguls. Mamoulian always recalled Eastman's gestures on his return visits to Rochester. "Inside this cover there was this curiosity, this interest, this striving for perfection—and real warmth. But he didn't slobber."

Nicolas Slonimsky

On 31 October 1923 "George Eastman Kodak Rochester" received a telegram from Southampton, England: SAILED HAPPY RETURNING ROCHESTER SLONIMSKY COACH WITH ME REGARDS GREETINGS ROSING. This meant that Rosing had found his American Opera coach and accompanist in Nicolas Slonimsky, age thirty, whose working English vocabulary when he alighted at Rochester's New York Central Station consisted of "yes," "please," and "thank you." But Slonimsky could still take conducting lessons from Rochester Philharmonic director Albert

Coates who, having been born and raised in St Petersburg, spoke Russian fluently. Slonimsky was well known to Rosing, having toured France, Belgium, and Spain with him in 1921 and 1922 as his accompanist. Slonimsky was born in St. Petersburg in 1894. As an adolescent he aspired to be, among other things, a novelist, revolutionary poet, literary critic, mathematician, Hebrew scholar, speculative philosopher, chess master, and economist and so, in his own words, "[He] wrote out his future biography accordingly, setting out his death date as 1967, but survived." Instead, he lived to age 101 as concert pianist, conductor, musicologist, and author of numerous books on music.

By fall 1923 an act from *The Barber of Seville* was being used as incidental entertainment with the silent films in the theater, three times daily for six days each week. In November 1924 the American Opera Company presented its first full public performance, *Pagliacci*, and by 1926 was producing a season of seven performances. "The formula for an American Opera Company is obvious," says Slonimsky with a pinch of irony. "Get four Russians and assign them roles—Rosing is producer, Mamoulian stage director, Coates conductor, Slonimsky coach." And it worked. Eastman liked the boisterous Russians and forgave their antics. When Joseph Press wanted a new instrument, Eastman gave him $6000 to buy one through Harold Gleason. Press later confided to Gleason that he had picked it up for $4000 and pocketed the change. After agonizing as to where his loyalties lay, Gleason told Eastman what had happened. "I'm glad you told me, Harold, but Press is Russian [sic]. These people have different standards than we Americans. He doesn't look on that as stealing. He sees it as a good business deal." Gleason, who had overheard an enormous row with Arthur Alexander over what he considered a much more minor transgression, was astonished. The only thing Eastman didn't quite understand about the Russians was how they could be completely *exhausted* after teaching one or two classes at the school.

Rosing taught a class in "mental training" at the Eastman School which began with the recitation of the incantation "Every day in every way we are getting better and better." He then instructed his class to flex the muscles of their brains. When Mamoulian pointed out that there were no muscles in the brain, Rosing retorted, "Nonsense, if there were no muscles in the brain, we couldn't make a mental effort." Radio broadcasting was the latest miracle of the age; Eastman and newspaper publisher Frank Gannett were arranging a hookup with the new station WHAM which would broadcast concerts from Kilbourn Hall and the Eastman Theatre. So Rosing included "mental radio" in his course as a natural extension of wireless communication. Rosing's own memory needed lots of propping: when he sang lead roles in *Faust* and other operas, he planted scraps of paper with the words of the recitatives hidden in the scenery. This worked fine until an unsuspecting stagehand removed all the cue cards and Rosing had no recourse but to repeat, with assorted facial grimaces, the first line of an aria over and over and over again.

Slonimsky's Perfect Pitch

"George Eastman," Slonimsky wrote in his autobiography, *Perfect Pitch*, "was a perfect prototype of an American philanthropist as American millionaires are portrayed in European fiction…. He was the first American millionaire whose hand I ever shook," Slonimsky recalled in his ninety-fourth year when he returned to Rochester to receive an honorary degree. Eastman's was a good firm handshake accompanied by a "limited smile," and it came after Slonimsky had finished playing the piano for Sunday breakfast at Eastman's home. Since Harold Gleason played the organ at St. Paul's Episcopal Church on Sunday mornings, alternate arrangements were made for a trio consisting of Joseph Press, first cellist of the Rochester Philharmonic Orchestra and Kilbourn Quartet, accompanied by a violinist, plus Slonimsky on piano. The trio played on the second floor balcony overlooking the conservatory where, Slonimsky said, "[He] could see us but we couldn't see him."

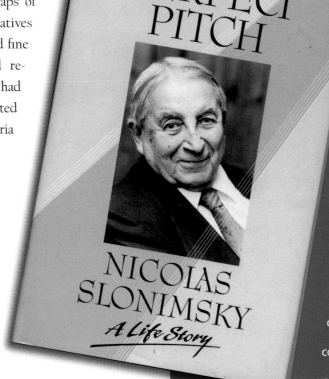

PERFECT PITCH

NICOLAS SLONIMSKY

A Life Story

The 1925
production of
Carmen involved
Mamoulian,
Horgan, Rosing,
and Slonimsky.
The Rochester
American Opera
Company was the
first opera group
at the Eastman
School.

Roman à Clef

In addition to the boisterous Russians, there was the American Paul Horgan, age twenty, who came to take singing lessons but soon found himself assistant to Mamoulian in composing and designing scenery. Horgan later attained fame as a novelist and historian.

These incidents and more are delightfully captured in Paul Horgan's first novel, *The Fault of Angels*, which won the Harper Prize in 1933. A *roman à clef*, the novel depicts a very provincial Rochester (Horgan calls it "Dorchester") suddenly descended upon by eccentrics and exotics from every corner of Europe, lured to upstate New York by Eastman and his musical creation. He also described an Eastman-like tycoon named "Henry Ganson" in a chapter entitled "Imperator Americanus." The coming of the Eastman School to Rochester brought a cultural clash in this period, and the city that emerged from it was never quite the same. Horgan recorded "the exhilaration of a Rochester winter" and "the excitement of the music" as well as the first nights of the opera when the wives of the university professors "had the courage to look splendidly dowdy." He sketched the "cluster of cheap little restaurants that gathered around the Theater" and the Corner Club, where theater people congregated from the 1920s to the 1950s.

There was, according to Horgan, a "severe tradition in the Theater of how many heads had fallen under the knife…. More people had been fired from their jobs than seemed possible." At this moment in the novel, the Eastman character walks into his music school "looking down at the floor and along the walls to see if all was neat and clean. 'Good morning, sir,' [a Horgan character] said, …not knowing the style in which to accom-

modate a millionaire in his own building…Mr. [Eastman] waved, …clapped his hat on and went out, his stomach preceding him a trifle, his arms hanging loose in the flapping open folds of his top-coat…. Winter with its withdrawal of color from the city had made everything resemble a photograph of itself. The streets had the familiarity of postcards."

In the novel, Horgan's character "spends his life on a series of planes…with marvelous Russians who spoke a special language of the intellect, with Americans of his own generation who passed casually in and out of his days, …with Americans in the arts, with Englishmen, with Mr. [Eastman], austere and solitary, a whole society unto himself…." Elsewhere, he observes "an unhappy conductor obliged to conduct 'Hearts and Flowers' for the movie after having been an opera conductor."

The Corner Club

Walking into the Corner Club in the 1920s, one was as likely to overhear French, German, Spanish, Russian, Hungarian, Italian, or British English spoken as to hear American English. It was indeed symptomatic of the loss of Rochester's provincialism because of the international stew that George Eastman concocted by hiring so many foreigners to work in the school, theater, and orchestra. Founded in 1921 in an eight-room house on the southwest corner of Grove Place and Windsor Street, the Corner Club was limited to 100 men and women with interest in the arts, especially music. Mrs. Thompson, the live-in caretaker, prepared the eatables. Tea was available to members without notice, while a forty-cent lunch or a sixty-cent *plat du jour* dinner could be ordered in advance. The club disbanded about 1950, shortly after some of its members were arrested by Governor Thomas Dewey's police force for harboring and playing slot machines.

George Eastman waves to members of the Budapest Chamber Orchestra who are serenading him.

The Kodak studio on the top floor of the Eastman School Annex was where early two-color Kodachrome films and stills were made.

so fast that you couldn't be surprised about anything." But Eastman liked the performance, and the ballet company was born. Under Botsford the company grew from six to 100 participants before the Eastman Theatre took it over in 1924.

Rush Rhees was a bit nervous, Botsford thought, that the Baptist trustees of his university would not understand a dancing school. Indeed Rhees and Eastman were meeting opposition to movies scheduled for Sunday, films with too much suggestive sex, and with the Wednesday Philharmonic concerts which conflicted with the mid-week services in many of Rochester's churches. To accommodate this conflict, Eastman changed his own mid-week musicales from Thursday to Wednesday night so that the Philharmonic could play in the Eastman Theatre on Thursday night. It still does. Rhees, an ordained Baptist minister himself, actually presided over the orderly secularization of the University of Rochester. He never would have gotten $51 million from Eastman if he had not.

Eastman Theatre Ballet

In 1923 the Eastman Theatre Ballet was created by the London-trained Enid Knapp [Botsford], a young Rochesterian then studying classical ballet in New York. Seeing possibilities in the new theater, she persuaded Arthur Alexander to engage a New York company for a week. Mission accomplished, "I went," she would recall. "I was sort of leaping out of the theater. Strangely enough, I never saw Mr. Alexander again….That was the fascinating part about the Eastman Theatre: things were happening

MARTHA GRAHAM

Backstage at the Eastman Theatre and School during the years 1925 and 1926, one of the most important artistic events in the history of America was quietly taking shape. It began with a 1911 performance by dance pioneer Ruth St. Denis, who, along with her rival Isadora Duncan, had broken with classical ballet. Martha Graham saw that performance and never forgot it. In 1916, at age twenty-two (old for an apprentice dancer), she joined the Denishawn Company, founded in 1914 by St. Denis and her husband, Ted Shawn. When, in 1925, after years of performing between animal acts with the Greenwich Village Follies, Graham was hired by Rouben Mamoulian to train dancers for routines between-movie acts at the Eastman Theatre, the only technique she knew was Denishawn. But soon Ted Shawn was demanding $500 for the use of his material. Martha refused, partly because of her innate penury and partly because she didn't have $500. Instead she created a wholly new technique for her Rochester students. (In later years Graham charged students $500 to use her material and technique when away from her supervision.)

Up to that moment, the Eastman dance students had as their teacher a restrained and proper but earthy Swedish nature dancer, Esther Gustafson, who thought that eyeliner was an instrument of the devil. In order to shock the students into a new attitude, Graham appeared in a clinging red silk kimono with a long slit up each leg and full makeup.

David Diamond

In April 1926 "Martha Graham and Dance Group," a trio from the Eastman School—Evelyn Sabin, Thelma Biracree, and Betty MacDonald—performed 18 numbers in New York City. A month later the same trio performed *Flute of Krishna*, choreographed—in those days they said "arranged"—by Graham, in the Eastman Theatre. The twelve-minute *Flute* was filmed in the Kodak studio on the top floor of the Eastman School using a new two-color "Kodachrome" process. Despite a studio of her own, all the students she could want, and a generous attitude on the part of both Howard Hanson and Eastman, when it was time to renew her contract, Graham got as far as signing "M," then put the pen back down on Hanson's desk. That is the story Martha relates in her memoir, *Blood Memory*. Composer David Diamond, then an Eastman School student, says that during this last exchange, Graham threw a telephone book at Hanson.

Except for *Flute of Krishna*, Graham left few traces of her year and a half at Eastman. What Rochesterians did not understand, she records, was that dance was going to develop into an art and not remain an entertainment in the spirit of Radio City Music Hall (founded a decade later) and that all her Rochester superiors wanted were "revues suitable for the Eastman Theatre."

And so Martha Graham returned to Manhattan. There she continued developing her revolutionary new dance language and stage aesthetic. Finally she became, perhaps, the most important and influential American dancer ever.

Paramount-Publix

The advent of talkies is usually blamed for the demise of the Eastman Theatre as a movie house in the late 1920s. However, other factors were at work. Hardly had the theater opened when a demand was heard to annul its tax exemption on the grounds that admission was paid for movies. Eastman argued that "listeners" were being educated: they paid their tuition at the gate and the theater was essentially a laboratory for the music school. The corporation counsel for the city agreed but then the state tax commission disagreed. "It will be an awful blow if they tax the Theatre," Eastman wrote. The Rochester press and general public were incensed that, as one citizen wrote, "After all the things that you have done for Rochester and are continually doing, it seems too bad that any of these good things should be criticized." Eastman himself was so incensed that he declared, "If they succeed in taxing this theatre I will go down with hammer and nails and close the doors myself."

However, the state tax commissioner held that the commission's "opinion is not binding on the assessors of the city of Rochester." So Eastman asked to have the assessors and tax commissioners "go to a full performance at three, seven, or nine o'clock, when they will hear the orchestra." In the end the assessors bowed to what another citizen called "the unusual regard in which Mr. Eastman is held by the rank and file, and their confidence in his leadership."

Taxes were not the only problem the Eastman Theatre faced in the late 1920s. Vincent Lenti, Eastman School of Music historian, has written that "up until this time the Eastman Theatre had simply 'out-classed' all the movie houses in town." With the building in 1928 of the RKO Palace and the equally palatial Rochester (later Loew's) Theater, which boasted that it was "air cooled," all this changed. One result of the air-cooled claim was that the Eastman Theatre suddenly sprouted nozzles where the walls met the ceiling in the second balcony as complaints about that area's stuffiness mounted. Those nozzles supplying a 1920s type of air conditioning remained in place until 2009.

Most important, since Hollywood studios had their own theaters, the Eastman had difficulty obtaining the best films from booking agencies. In 1922 Eastman, along with other Rochester industrialists, formed the Regorson Corporation on behalf of the university to get first-rate films for the Eastman as well as the Piccadilly and Regent theaters. As the theater began to fail financially, Eastman's desperate petty economies in his $17.5-million complex increased. He chastised Arthur See for sending out the bulletin with a two-cent (first class) stamp. Was there a way, he wondered, short of plunging the theater into total darkness, of reducing the $2.88-per-hour cost of operating the

Air Conditioning?

The Eastman Theatre claimed to have the latest and newest of everything when it opened in 1922. And indeed, it had the largest theater organ ever built, the longest marquee in the world, and a seminal kind of air conditioning that was installed a few years later. But the second balcony remained hot; so under Paramount-Publix management, the system was expanded by adding nozzles that allowed cold air to be blown and circulated. Unfortunately, the nozzles covered the decorative frieze where wall met ceiling. With the 2009 renovation, a new heating and air-conditioning system has been installed, retiring radiators and nozzles. After eighty years, the decorative frieze is once again apparent in all of its unharmed glory.

chandelier? Finally he decided with extreme reluctance that "the Eastman Theatre has not made a financial go of it" and in 1928 signed a ten-year lease with Paramount's Publix Corporation to run the movie part. The lease provided twenty days each season be reserved for concerts and an additional three days in the spring for the Metropolitan Opera. Publix immediately started to redecorate the theater in the manner of a glitzy movie palace until artists, architects and the general public, who by this time had grown to love "their theatre," petitioned Eastman in droves.

This did not signal a "failure of the musical enterprise," the eternal optimist assured everyone. "There is every prospect that the apparent setback will be turned into a bigger success than we have heretofore had any hope of," referring to the Civic Music Association which was being formed to turn the old Subscribers Association of 600 orchestra supporters into 10,000 members. But Eastman did write to university officials:

> I am not a theatre expert but as an observer of human nature and after hearing the comments of the people who made a habit of going to the theatre, I am convinced the new curtains take away more old patrons than they add new ones. It used to be customary with residents to take visitors to the theatre to show it as an outstanding piece of theatre art, whether they liked the movies or not.

"I hope the talk of redecorating is only gossip," an agonized Lawrence White wrote in 1929, "and that you will use your influence to keep the decorations as they are at present." "My dear Lawrence White," a resigned Eastman replied, "Our contract with the Publix people prevents their making any permanent changes without consent....In order to 'pep up' the interior they have hung a red curtain in the proscenium arch that would break your heart. It nearly did that to mine and I am not so sensitive as you are. They talk about covering the murals with

hangings to regulate the sound of the talkies. If they decide to do this we will try to mitigate the horror of their color scheme." Eastman even offered to pay one-half of the expenses if Publix changed those offensive red curtains, "a glaring atrocity, ...for something that would pass the approval of McKim, Mead & White." But after three years as a movie palace, except for the Thursday night concerts, Publix broke its lease and the university resumed administrative control.

"The one matter of grave concern in all of this," historian Vincent Lenti has written, "was the future of the Rochester Philharmonic Orchestra." As we shall see, the community rallied and the RPO is going strong in 2010.

Madalena

One element that George Eastman considered vital to the success of the Eastman Theatre as movie house was the seven ornate polished brass display cases for advertising posters that flanked the theater's entrances. The mass-produced posters supplied by the movie houses would not do. The theater management and Kodak advertising department searched portfolios and settled on the Italian born Batiste Madalena, then in his early twenties and a recent graduate of Mechanics Institute (now the Rochester Institute of Technology). Eastman issued only one directive—that the paintings be visible from passing trolleys. And so with bold and colorful tempera on poster board, Madalena painted more than 1400 fantastic posters especially for the Eastman Theatre between 1924 and 1928. When the Paramount-Publix management took over, it had no use for a poster artist, and hundreds of original Madalenas were simply tossed. On a cold rainy night, Madalena was riding his bicycle home when he saw the soggy mess of his handiwork scattered along Swan Street. He gathered up as many as he could and took them home to dry and press them. In the 1970s Steven Katten, a visiting filmmaker from Los Angeles, saw one of the salvaged posters and eventually bought the whole collection.

What I am personally interested in…is the making of a musical city. By that I mean where the inhabitants love to listen to good music. —George Eastman

A symphony orchestra was part of Eastman's grand plan to galvanize Rochester into an instant musical center. Neither a school of music nor providing instruments for school children was enough. Once the music idea took root, his energy and imagination were focused on the project in its entirety. "The great project for training listeners is in the Eastman Theatre," he would say in his own living room at the organizational meeting of the Subscribers Association to support a new Rochester Philharmonic Orchestra. The music Eastman had in mind all along was "orchestral music which, outside of opera, is the most expensive form of music that there is. The great orchestras of the country are only in the large cities," he noted.

It is estimated that it costs about $2.50 for every listener at each orchestra performance…far beyond what can be collected at the box office and the deficits…are made up by a comparatively small group

Sir Eugene Goossens, conductor of the Rochester Philharmonic Orchestra from 1923–1931, became regarded by many as one of the great conductors of the early twentieth century.

of citizens who perhaps scarcely realize that they are paying from $1.00 to $1.50 for each person who hears the orchestra. This is really an economic crime; especially because a vast majority of the people who hear orchestras are already interested in music and therefore the music is being furnished not so much for education but merely for the gratification of those who are already music lovers…. It is impossible to reduce the cost of orchestra music. You must have the men; you must pay the wages; you must have the rehearsals; and you must have the director…. Now the only way it seems possible to reduce this tremendous cost of $2.50 per listener is by increasing the number of listeners. It is with that object in view that the Eastman Theatre has been built and in that theatre, if things go on as they are now going, it will be possible to reduce that cost of $2.50 per listener to $0.25.

Eastman's reasoning was based on the statistics that instead of playing to the usual 150,000 people per year (or 15,000 different individuals), a movie orchestra could play five hours a day to two million people a year. His "theory [was] that the people of Rochester who are not interested particularly in music, most of whom never go to hear orchestral music, will as they hear this music day after day come gradually to an appreciation of its beauty and the place it ought to occupy in their lives…. Music is something which belongs in every life and the people who have missed it have missed it because they have had no opportunity to

Conductor Arthur Alexander on
the roof of the annex with
orchestra members:

1—Harry Shatz, violin

2—Lucille Johnson Bigelow, harp

3—George Neidinger, violin

4—Emory Remington, trombone

5—Hermann Rudin, viola

6—William G. Street, drums

7—Harry Waterhouse, drums

8—George Waterhouse, drums

make it a part of their lives." This "theater" part of his "great project," both in terms of raising money through movies for the school and in training listeners who would support a symphony orchestra, would never be understood by the conservatory-trained and -oriented first director of the Eastman School.

Even his friends were doubters. "You may not know it, but many sneered at the theatre idea and jeered the university for 'running a theatre,' " George W. Todd wrote Eastman in 1925, "and I must confess that I could not understand how you had the courage to attempt it, but the laugh is on the 'doubting Thomases.' The plan is a winner—it works." Todd and his brother, Libanus, had developed a successful business producing special check-writing paper. George Todd would later become centrally involved with Eastman in moving the university to a new campus by the Genesee River. Harvey Padelford, Eastman's chauffeur, thought that Todd was "Mr. Eastman's twin—in looks and through their mutual interests of music, hunting, and business." Indeed, when Todd took his wife for a spin in their roadster, tongues wagged that Mr. Eastman had a new love interest. The Todds wondered too why Eastman insisted on such severe architecture for the

medical school and university, since Goethe called architecture "frozen music," and Eastman was so fond of music.

"Our musical enterprise is rather an ambitious one," Eastman said with typical understatement, "having in view the making of a truly musical community. To do this it is as necessary to educate listeners as it is…performers…. It is fairly easy to employ skillful musicians," he explained to the *The New York Times* in 1920. "It is impossible

to buy an appreciation of music. Yet, without appreciation, without a presence of a large body of people who understand music and who get joy out of it, any attempt to develop the musical resources of any city is doomed to failure. Because in Rochester we realize this, we have undertaken a scheme for building musical capacity on a large scale from childhood…. The symphony orchestra will have as its foundation the motion picture orchestra which will be augmented somewhat for the eight, ten, or twelve concerts…of the season," Eastman noted. In 1930 there were only seventeen professional symphony orchestras in the entire country and Rochester's had already achieved remarkable distinction, considering its brief life. Despite gloomy predictions for a symphony in a community the size of Rochester and despite many crises, mostly financial, the Rochester Philharmonic Orchestra is alive and well in 2010. Eastman thought people would appreciate only undertakings that they paid for. "This was a keynote in the character of the man," said Katharine Whipple, wife of the founding dean of the new School of Medicine and Dentistry. "He was willing to help anybody if they'd help themselves but he wasn't going to spoon feed anybody. This idea of the Philharmonic—he gave it to the

Katharine Whipple (standing), wife of the founding dean of the new School of Medicine and Dentistry, with George Eastman

city for a certain length of time. If they wanted it, they had to support it themselves."

The February 1919 day that Eastman learned about the orchestra under-writing committee over lunch at Kodak Office, he told Todd (and Rhees in a letter) that his plan was "to devote the music hall to motion pictures six days of the week, putting all of the profits into the music hall orchestra." Todd must have been amazed at this concept, so different from the way Rochesterians had been used to raising money to support their orchestras for the past half century. In Florida, Rhees was startled to learn that the university was to have a movie theater. "The minor Medici of Rochester," Howard Hanson said later, "were not particularly pleased by having Mr. Eastman come in. They had been the leaders in the arts and music. Suddenly this man comes in with all of his money and plants a great music school in the middle of the city and a great symphony orchestra there and an opera company. Well, who was *he* taking over culture in Rochester? What did *he* know about music? There was quite of bit of that kind of talk when I came [in 1924] although I don't think anyone turned down an invitation to his home."

THE EASTMAN THEATRE ORCHESTRA

Eastman's plans went on apace. There could be two orchestras, he decided, a "small" orchestra of about fifty-five to accompany the silent movies and an augmented symphony of about ninety for concerts. Although, Eastman said, "as I explained to Mr. Todd, the whole of my plan could be carried out without having a big orchestra at all…. Having the [symphony] orchestra will depend wholly upon the support of the community." Eastman was willing, he told Todd, "to have the hall used in the way indicated by community support." This matter would have to be taken up by a citizens committee such as Todd had formed. "I told him that it would take a lot more money than had been heretofore raised by the small group [of supporters]." Todd was not to be dissuaded by financial hurdles: "He said he thought the town ought to have an orchestra and that he did not think there would be any trouble about raising the money." Eastman began nosing around among his music friends and found that "several people here are more enthusiastic about the big orchestra than I expected." So he had another office lunch with Todd, who immediately said, "We ought to go to work now." But Eastman wanted to make sure Todd knew what he was biting off. "I told him it would be necessary in addition to the underwriting for the old [Dossenbach] orchestra to raise about $25,000 for preparatory work and $30,000 or $40,000 after that. He said the underwriting ought to be for three years and I left him with the understanding that he would have an interview with Mr. and Mrs. Klingenberg this afternoon in order, as he said, to get enthused." Soon Todd's group would become the Subscribers Association, dedicated to the support of the new Rochester Philharmonic Orchestra. In 1930 when the core Eastman Theatre Orchestra was renamed the Rochester Civic Orchestra, the supporters became the Civic Music Association. Since 1975, the organization and both the core and augmented orchestra have been called the Rochester Philharmonic Orchestra or RPO.

Eastman must have expected Todd to opt for the full philharmonic orchestra because Eastman had already hired Alexander to be his "general music director and advisor." The ensemble of approximately seventy players, far above the proficiency level of the usual movie orchestra, made possible a distinguished orchestral faculty at the school, which in remarkably short order spun off a student orchestra of exceptional quality. The school, theater, and orchestra were so closely integrated in people's minds that Howard Hanson once remarked, "If the doorman in the foyer of the Theatre sneezes the entire opera department (on the top floor of the annex) catches cold." The theater orchestra was increased to philharmonic size by adding the string members of Eastman's quartet plus instrumentalists from the school and community. Some of the orchestra's cost in the early years was absorbed by the theater and the rest by the Subscribers Association ($50,000 for the first season of 1923-1924, for example). But once it was clear that "talkies" would put theater orchestras out of business, the Subscribers Association of 600 members (already up from the 100 or so who supported the old Dossenbach Orchestra) expanded in 1930 to a Civic Music Association of 10,000 contributors.

Despite public perceptions that the school, theater, and orchestra are one entity, they have always been separate financially and administratively. William L. Cahn, author of *Rochester's Orchestra 1968–1995*, explains that from the beginning, the theater including the theater orchestra was under separate management, with the university holding title. After

Venus de Milo with Arms

1929 the orchestra was turned over to the Civic Music Association while the theater continued under the university.

Eastman had ambitious ideas for the Rochester Philharmonic Orchestra and the impact it was going to have on the community, particularly on young people. While commenting that other symphonies played to only 100,000-150,000 people per year even in larger cities, he went on to say, "In connection with the motion pictures we expect that our orchestra will play to ten times that number. Our theory is that by giving them music that is not over their heads at first we can gradually educate the motion picture goers to a high degree of appreciation for good music." This view probably accounts for the eclectic nature of the early philharmonic programs where Rudolf Friml was sandwiched between Mozart and Wagner, and it was considered prudent to avoid taxing the audience by playing but one movement of a symphony.

Lucille Johnson Bigelow Harrison Rosenblum was the original harpist of the Rochester Philharmonic Orchestra and first harp teacher at the Eastman School of Music. She played as soloist in a chamber group conducted by Coates and in recital with the Kilbourn Quartet. Goossens wrote *Suite for Flute, Violin and Harp, Opus 6* for her, which debuted in 1923 at Eastman's home.

The international trio of Horgan, Mamoulian, and Rosing formed a cult of adoration for "Venus de Milo with arms...our universally admired, golden-tressed harpist" who had several "transient husbands." Slonimsky wrote that Lucille's "blonde halo and cerulean eyes formed complementary colors to her golden harp which she fingered ever so innocently."

The three of them made festive occasions of her weekend departures for her Buffalo home, accompanying her to the train station and adorning her with costume jewelry. They wore monocles, spoke German and clicked their heels to impress onlookers that she was a silent film star and they were her directors. Once they "staged a party in a Rochester coffee shop. We placed a boxful of matches inside the birthday cake" and lit it so the cake "blew up with an impressive bang. We were asked to leave."

A half-century later, Slonimsky sent his "adored lady of the harp" some recordings and "Dear Nicolai" received the reply:

> *You really are a genius, even though you ceased being an unrecognized one years ago!*
> *... How I laughed when I heard the 'ads': after so many years I remembered them*
> *perfectly and they brought you closer to me and to the wonderful times we had together.*

ARTHUR ALEXANDER

Born in New Zealand in 1891, Arthur Alexander had been sent at an early age to England, where he garnered many prizes as a student, debuted in Vienna in 1912, did a little composing, but made his greatest reputation as a pianoforte teacher. Alexander's first act in Rochester was to bring in a new first violinist, Arthur Hartmann. He would shortly personify the ecstasies of electrifying music and agonies of financial and personal difficulties which Eastman would face in this new breed of European musician coming to conservative Rochester. The town would be alternately amazed, diverted and scandalized by Hartmann and his ilk. Hartmann and Alexander, "the newcomers among the musicians," as Eastman called them, would also represent a threat to Eastman's old violinist, Hermann Dossenbach. Eventually the Dossenbach Quintette would be eased out of their twice-weekly musicale schedule at Eastman's home although they still played occasionally for Eastman or were sent by him to Kodak Park. The quintet was replaced by the new Kilbourn Quartet formed from imported European musicians, who also would hold the principal chairs in their respective sections of the philharmonic and teach at the new music school. Some theorized that the school was built so that Eastman's personal quartet would be gainfully employed.

In 1918 Arthur Alexander, then just Eastman's "musical expert," had been delighted to have "things arranged so satisfactorily, and to have the opportunity of…adding my modest bit to the building up of a deeper musical feeling in Rochester." Alexander and his wife were so taken with Rochester that they decided to live there and commute in reverse: "He will spend three days of each week in New York studying the work of various directors," Eastman told his friend Otto Kahn, chairman of the board of the Metropolitan Opera, in asking Kahn's permission for Alexander to attend rehearsals of the Metropolitan Orchestra. But modest Alexander was not. And he was always in debt, always asking for advances, and thus possessed of that improvident personality sure to eventually irritate Eastman. Then one evening on Mary Mulligan's porch during the fall of

During summer months, the music patrons of Rochester met on the porches of Dr. and Mrs. Mulligan's house (shown at right as it looks today) to discuss the orchestra situation. Often, when discussions were over, George Eastman was observed vaulting over a porch railing before walking the block to his home.

1919, after Dossenbach had turned down the offer to lead the movie orchestra, Alexander proposed to Eastman that he might direct the movie orchestra in addition to the symphony orchestra. Eastman began warming to the idea, talking it over with Todd, whom he had appointed a co-director of the Eastman Theatre along with himself, Rhees, and Klingenberg. He did not realize that Alexander's motive was not just "the building up of a deeper musical feeling" but also mustering the movie conductor's salary in addition to his already agreed-upon symphony conductor's salary. Eastman was dumbfounded. "If you expected to get additional compensation for it you should have said so on the porch." Setting up a staff and deciding who paid whose salary in such a new venture was an amorphous proposition. Alexander was already being paid $30,000 (compared to Gleason's $2,500); $20,000 was furnished by Eastman with $10,000 to come from the Subscribers Association once the orchestra season was under way.

In addition to having charge of the music in the new auditorium, Alexander was to direct Eastman's Sunday and Thursday musicales at Eastman's home. Eastman expected one thing from their agreement, Alexander another. "I am much interested in your musical evenings," Alexander professed, "and even if I do not appear myself at every one…we may make some interesting and perhaps unusual programs." That was hardly enough for Eastman. Then on another evening, the Aeolian organ in Eastman's conservatory squeaked, groaned, and finally collapsed. "Why didn't you check it during rehearsal?" Eastman asked, only to wonder further if there had been any rehearsal. "I am not your personal organist," Alexander replied angrily (and indeed Eastman already had procured the services of Harold Gleason to fill that role) and went on to demand that Eastman

"define my duties." In a third draft of a letter to Alexander, Eastman wrote:

> In view of your saying last night that you were not my private organist, that you had come to the conclusion you could not play the piano quartets; that music in the evening [at Eastman's home] was an afterthought after you came last year; your evident feeling that you were not responsible for last Sunday's fiasco; and our agreement that you should sing only once a month, I am at a loss to comply with your request; so I will state what I wish to accomplish…:

> The primary object of all music at my house is to enable me to listen to good music under conditions which I control…. All other considerations, such as the pleasure of my friends or the musicians, the building up of a fine quartet, and the affording of an opportunity to musicians, are all quite secondary, desirable as they may be. If you cannot look at this matter straight and feel that my position is reasonable the situation will be impossible and that is why I am writing you this decided letter. Personally I have become very fond of you.

Eastman found himself confronting an enormous artistic ego. Generally, the old-school Rochester musicians were courteous and subservient. Eastman wrote Alexander, "I am quite willing to admit that you are a heaven born musical genius but that does not interest me in this particular enterprise [the music at Eastman's home] unless I get pure pleasure out of it…."

> I have given you an opportunity to make a career which you have failed to appreciate and take advantage of…. You never seem to realize that to make you a conductor is not the main object of the great musical enterprise with which you have been connected. The main object…is to establish an orchestra here in the city of Rochester of the very highest order, and to have it so conducted as to be a great influence in spreading the love of music among the

Lily PONS, *coloratura soprano*

Paul ROBESON, *baritone*

Feodor CHALIAPIN, *operatic bass*

PARADE *of* MASTERS

ARTISTS WHO

PERFORMED IN

CONCERT AND

AS ORCHESTRA

SOLOISTS AT THE

EASTMAN THEATRE

1922–1932

people of the town. I was quite sure you had the musical ability…but I had doubts as to whether you had the other qualities…. Lack of cooperation from you is the chief reason for my conviction that it is impossible to have you in the organization…. You have been occupying one of the key positions which require breadth of vision, unselfishness, and cooperation in a high degree. You have lamentably failed in all of these…. I blame myself that notwithstanding my wide experience in selecting men to take charge of matters in which I am not an expert I did not see this before and discourage you from making an experiment which was bound to fail.

Eastman rewrote his letter to Alexander three times and ended on a positive note about being "confident that there are other uses to which you can put your remarkable talents which ought to satisfy you and would benefit others. If I can help you on any such line I shall always be glad to do so." One point that did not make the final draft was "Your [Alexander's] statement that most people are afraid of me is a matter of opinion but…you certainly have never been afraid to ask me for anything you wanted."

Harold Gleason never understood how Alexander could throw away such an incredible salary. "He had a conduc-

torship. Mr. Eastman made him conductor of the orchestra, the symphony orchestra and even the theater orchestra just so he could practice. He wasn't a conductor before. He had opportunities for singing, recitals, accompanying himself, accompanying other people," Gleason continued. "He lived in an historic 1830s mansion. He had servants. He was living like a king and he was a favorite of George Eastman's. He walked out of all that just like this."

The combination of Alexander's complex finances and a messy personal life, his refusal to take Eastman's home musicales seriously as a part of his job, and his petulant and stormy attitude in general led to his contract not being renewed in 1923. By then the Rochester Philharmonic Orchestra and the Subscribers Association to support it had been officially organized. And so Alexander's opening concert of 28 March 1923 was also his farewell concert. "It was a very good program, well selected and well played," Eastman wrote. "The audience was very enthusiastic and bestowed its favors evenly upon Alexander and Klingenberg" (who had also been fired but as soloist played a Grieg piano concerto). In accordance with Eastman's request that concerts contain a work by Wagner, "Siegfried's Death" from *Die Götterdämmerung* was performed, followed by Victor Herbert's *Irish Rhapsody* to sweeten the musical menu. Rochester did not turn out in force to say hello and goodbye. "Unfortunately the house was only half full although the admission price was very low. Orchestra seats went for one dollar…. The overall deficit was $2,400." Eastman understood

Fritz KREISLER, *violinist*

Vladimir HOROWITZ, *pianist*

Anna PAVLOVA, *ballerina*

that ticket sales would not prevent operating deficits; hence his hope was that the movie profits plus the Subscribers Association would make up the shortfall.

Sometimes Eastman's musicians claimed he had no understanding of the "musical temperament." Eastman decided that temperament was a term used by these musicians to cover sheer laziness in not wanting to practice and consistently perform at their highest level. He felt that a musical contract was like any other contract and should be observed, and his intolerance, if any, Hanson said later, extended only to cases of bad faith or sloth. Eastman's one gripe with the Russians was their "laziness." Hanson suggested that if musicians wanted real examples of a "businesslike" attitude, they might consider such orchestral directors as Toscanini or Koussevitzky who would make Eastman seem relaxed and indulgent by contrast.

Alexander would not remember his five years in Rochester warmly; they are not mentioned in his biographical sketch in the *Grove Dictionary of Music and Musicians.* Nor did Alexander fare well after Rochester: years later Harold Gleason looked him up in Los Angeles, finding him on a side street on the second floor over a store. "There in a small studio he was giving voice lessons."

Arturo Toscanini conducted the New York Philharmonic Orchestra in the Eastman Theatre during the 1920s.

Myra HESS, *pianist*

Alexander LEVENTON, *concertmaster and violinist*

Efrem ZIMBALIST, *violinist*

PARADE *of* MASTERS

Eastman was not discouraged. "It will take time," he wrote, "but I have little doubt that eventually if we get a conductor who appeals to the public we will be able to work up a strong clientele for these local orchestral concerts."

ALBERT COATES

Albert Coates (1882-1953), born of a Russian mother and English father and the youngest of seven sons, was sent to England for schooling, but returned as bookkeeper to the family busi-

Serge Koussevitzky, known as "the first Russian conductor," began conducting in Europe in 1901. From 1924 to 1949, he was the renowned director of the Boston Symphony Orchestra, a golden era for that ensemble. During the 1927-1928 season, Koussevitzky conducted the Rochester Philharmonic Orchestra in the Eastman Theatre.

ness in St. Petersburg. Eschewing that business career, Coates entered the Leipzig Conservatory in 1902 at age twenty to study the cello, piano, and conducting. Between 1906 and 1914 he conducted the Elberfeld, Mannheim, and Dresden Operas, was invited to conduct *Siegfried* in St. Petersburg in 1914, and was named principal conductor there for the next five years. He escaped with great difficulty during the Russian Revolution to become one of the regular conductors of the London season. Since 1913 Coates had been prominent in England for his Wagner performances at Covent Garden and in New York, where he conducted the Philharmonic Society and the Symphony Society Orchestras.

Coates buttonholed Eastman at a Carnegie Hall gala in 1922, begging him to provide finances for soloists for the London Symphony, an amateur orchestra (in the sense that the musicians were not paid) of 100 members that Coates conducted. "It is impossible to get support for music in England," Coates explained, "the taxes are too heavy." Eastman said he had too many musical enterprises going in Rochester, but to try again. "Your name is so well known in England that we feel that you somehow belong to us too," Coates wrote Eastman in a follow-up begging letter in February 1923. Eastman again demurred, but after checking with Harry Harkness Flagler, prominent patron of music in New York, invited Coates to Rochester via transatlantic cable in May that succinctly in eighteen lines presented Eastman's whole philosophy for his music "scheme" and read in part:

Albert Coates with George Eastman and his dog Herro

Come, Tell It to Coates...

To the wonderful
Eastman school of Music
with all my sympathy + interest
in your great work
Albert Coates
London April 1923

George Eastman often told enquiring art dealers that he wasn't a collector. But he collected people, selectively, for Kodak Park in the 1890s and for his great musical enterprises in the 1920s. One of his favorite new friends was the conductor and composer Albert Coates.

Eastman loved seeing people come to the Eastman Theatre. It was a matter of pride with him that the theater had a common entrance for all—orchestra, mezzanine, second balcony. He was delighted to see people affectionately touch and smooth carpets and hangings even if it meant a few fingerprints. He also collected humorous stories about his theater—some of them tinged with the ethnic slights of the day.

One he loved to retell was a conversation between two women who came for a concert: "Shurin, Mary, I always did enjoy *Tannhäuser*."

"Get along with you, that ain't *Tannhäuser*, thim's th' *Tales of Hoffmann*, of which I've heard before."

"I don't agree with you."

"Well we'll soon settle that for I saw a sign down in front where the musicians come in to show what they're playing. I'll go down and read it." So down the aisle she went only to return dejected, saying "Mary, we're both wrong. It do be the *Refrain from Spittin*."

Eastman grabbed the friend who told him the story by the arm: "Come, tell it to Coates," he said.

Yehudi MENUHIN,
violinist

Jascha HEIFETZ, *violinist*

Walter DAMROSCH,
conductor

PARADE of MASTERS

...OBJECT BEING TEACH MASSES APPRECIATE ORCHES-
TRA MUSIC AND FURNISH IT AT PRICES THEY CAN
AFFORD TO PAY. ORCHESTRA AVERAGES NOW 33,000
LISTENERS PER WEEK SOME WEEKS 60,000. EXPECT
RAISE AVERAGE TO 40 NEXT YEAR. IF PLAN SUCCEEDS
POSSIBLE FOR ALL CITIES MODERATE SIZE MAINTAIN
ORCHESTRAS WITHOUT ENORMOUS DEFICITS. ...
SALARY CONSIDERING EDUCATIONAL CHARACTER
LIBERAL BUT NONCOMPETITIVE NEW YORK

Four days of living at Eastman's home in early June followed for Coates, during which time he conducted a rehearsal with several high school orchestras and listened to over 300 school children "of astonishing ability" play the instruments Eastman had provided since 1919. An announcement on 11 June confirmed that Albert Coates was the new conductor. "On short acquaintance he confirmed all of your praise of him," Eastman told Flagler on 13 June, "and I really became much attached to him during the few days that he was a guest at my house."

Because of commitments to conduct Wagner's Ring Cycle at Covent Garden, Coates could not start the 1923-1924 season; so Eugene Goossens, another Briton, was engaged (on Coates's recommendation apparently) to conduct the fall concerts. Coates, however, was the music director for that first season. Coates engaged the musicians from Europe, although the Musicians Union in New York refused to let him import many of his first choices, claiming that musicians of equal ability could be found in this country. Vladimir Shavitch was engaged as a second the-

ater orchestra conductor, Victor Wagner having been hired in 1921. Also in June 1923, Eastman engaged Carnegie Hall for the Rochester Philharmonic Orchestra to debut there the following April under Coates's direction and confirmed that Vladimir Rosing would be coming "for our summer school, to make some experiments with opera material [students] which we have in our School. If it looks good, we want to include it [the opera material] in your afternoon concerts," Eastman wrote Goossens.

"Some of the critics said that it was very cheeky of us to present ourselves so soon," Eastman said after the Carnegie Hall debut of 7 April 1924. He made a big splash of the event, hired a special train to take the orchestra to and from New York and filled the first tier boxes with a number of luminaries, friends, and business acquaintances. Frank Seaman, Kodak's advertising agent, brought to his box a bevy of Russian expatriates including Prince Youssoupoff, who had achieved his greatest notoriety by his inviting Monk Rasputin to his castle and shooting him.

"The object in taking the orchestra down there was twofold," Eastman said. "First, to show the Rochester public it had a first-class orchestra, and second, to have a salutary effect on the musicians themselves":

> The splendid audience was most enthusiastic.... The effect on the orchestra has been excellent. The men got inside opinions from the many members of other orchestras who came around to the stage door.... As for myself, my experience to date has satisfied me that there are no

Guy Fraser HARRISON, *conductor and organist*

PARADE *of* MASTERS

Paul WHITE, *conductor and violinist*

Lawrence TIBBETT, *baritone*

conditions here that are obstacles to our having one of the finest orchestras in the country in a comparatively short time. We find no difficulty in getting men of the highest rank, or keeping them.... All the good ones have already renewed their contracts for another year.

He took the New York critics' verdicts with good grace. "You will see they range from highly commendatory in the *Post* and *New York American* to quite scornful in the *Herald Tribune*.... Of course the critics did not agree; it would have been unfortunate if they had. If they all agreed [with the rave reviews] the Rochester public would have thought there was some hocus-pocus about it; or if they all agreed [with the *Tribune*] it would have been depressing. As it is they feel that the criticisms are honest and tinged only by the personality of the critic." *Time* magazine's critic called Eastman's whole scheme "the world's greatest experiment in exchanging money for culture," which article Eastman sent Goossens with the note: "Your English friends may think it an indication of our real musical cultivation."

Vladimir Shavitch (above)

Eugene Goossens, third from left, and Victor Wagner, second from right (right)

Rhapsody in Kodachrome

Unlikely as it sounds, two musicians who performed 1931 to 1939 in what is today Kodak Hall invented the famous Kodachrome film that was marketed in 1935.

Leopold Damrosch Mannes, who married Rochesterian Evelyn Sabin of Martha Graham's company, would eventually return to music: composing, performing as a pianist, and serving as president of the family's Mannes College of Music in New York City.

Violinist Leopold Godowsky Jr, son of one of the world's great pianists, married George Gershwin's sister before moving to Rochester.

In 1916 Godoswky Jr and Mannes became acquainted as amateur photographers. They decided, in the all-things-are-possible haze of youth, to improve upon an early color process in their school physics laboratory.

Soon they were producing color plates in bathtubs and sinks. When their tired parents, musicians all, declined to finance further experimentation, the youngsters called upon George Eastman. He received them courteously but they never heard from him again.

Eventually, Dr. C. E. Kenneth Mees, director of Kodak Research Laboratories, provided the moonlighting scientists with equipment and supplies, seeing their work as a possible solution for amateur color film. In 1930 Mees moved his protégés to Rochester. At Kodak Park "those musicians" became known as "Man and God"; at the Eastman School where they

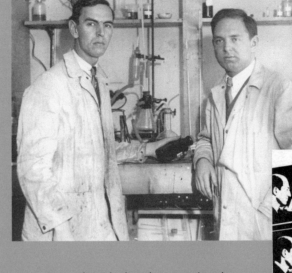

played chamber music, they were "those color experts." People who heard them play with the Rochester Philharmonic Orchestra wondered what Kodak was coming to, hiring a violinist and a pianist to do scientific research. Godowsky said that the newcomers made things worse as they "timed their developing by whistling, two beats a second, to Brahms' *C-Minor Symphony.*"

In 1935 Kodachrome motion picture film went on sale, followed by color slides. Byzantine in its complexity of development but breathtaking in its clarity and color, this was the color film that George Eastman had envisioned for amateurs to use in any camera.

Churchill in Rochester

In 1932 Winston Churchill (left, with his mother, Jennie) set off on an American lecture tour. In Rochester his lecture on economics, entitled "Gold," in the cavernous 3,300-seat Eastman Theatre, was sponsored by the Junior League, a service organization noted for its ability to raise funds for its projects. But people stayed away in droves, and the event failed as a fundraiser.

The 1930s were the depth of Churchill's obscurity. Behind him was the celebrity of soldier, war correspondent, politician, and First Lord of the Admiralty. Before him was great distinction. Churchill himself described the 1930s as a time when, having been saddled with the blame for the failure of the Gallipoli campaign in 1915, he had lost his job, his political party, and his appendix.

Reporter Henry Clune interviewed Churchill at his Rochester hotel the night before the 1932 talk. Answering the door in a tattered dressing gown, Scotch in hand, Churchill growled at Clune: "No, my mother was not born in Rochester. She was born in Brooklyn." Yet in 1941, when President Alan Valentine of the University of Rochester bestowed an honorary degree on him at commencement, the prime minister was happy to thank via transatlantic cable all of the residents of "the city of my mother's birth" assembled in the Eastman Theatre for the celebration. It was, after all, a time when England was desperate for Lend Lease and the entry of the United States into WWII.

Wherever his mother, the beautiful Jennie Jerome, was born, Churchill, through his Rochester grandmother, Clara Hall Jerome, was a New York State Iroquois—if only by a few drops.

Déjà vu....

Two future presidents of the Eastman Kodak Company, Thomas J. Hargrave (right, shaking the hand of George Eastman) and Frank W. Lovejoy, attended the Churchill lecture in 1932 in what would become Kodak Hall in 2009. So did John B. Pike, namesake and founder of the construction company that renovated and expanded the theater, 2004-2011.

EASTMAN KODAK COMPANY
ROCHESTER. N.Y.

January 29, 1932.

Genesee Valley Club,
421 East Avenue,
Rochester, New York.

Dear Sirs:

I previously sent you a post card requesting reservation of two seats for the Winston Churchill lecture. I will appreciate it if you will reserve two additional seats, making four in all for this event.

Yours very truly,

TJHargrave/n

Sir Eugene Goossens

Eugene Goossens (1893-1962) was a decade younger than Coates and commanded a smaller salary. A descendant of a long line of conductors and composers, and brother to several famous orchestral players, Goossens like Coates combined conducting with composition. He had trained at the Bruges Conservatory and Liverpool College of Music, became associated with Sir Thomas Beecham as conductor, and performed with the London Philharmonic String Quartet. His best known opera, *Judith*, was composed in 1929 while he was the conductor of the Rochester Philharmonic Orchestra and performed that same year in Covent Garden and in Rochester by Rosing's American Opera Company. Eastman sent A. J. "Jack" Warner II, music critic for Frank Gannett's *Times-Union* and son of architect J. Foster Warner, to England to clinch the deal with Goossens.

When Goossens and spouse arrived in 1923, Eastman gave them a banquet "which I cannot remember being equaled anywhere for lavish hospitality and sumptuous display," Goossens said later. "The decorations even featured miniature fountains which sprang from the center of the table." When the editor of *The Musical Digest* congratulated Eastman on a Goossens concert in 1923, Eastman commented: "The results have been very grati-

fying. The musical people seem to think we have now surprisingly good material and that Goossens has done almost a miracle with them." Goossens brought some good humor to his task, which may have helped him in his relations with Eastman. In fact, both Coates and Goossens would be at ease with their patron. "There existed between us a deep bond of affection," Goossens wrote in 1940. Coates addressed his employer as "Captain George" while Goossens wrote to "My dear friend." Eastman was both to the pair, even assuming the role of mar-

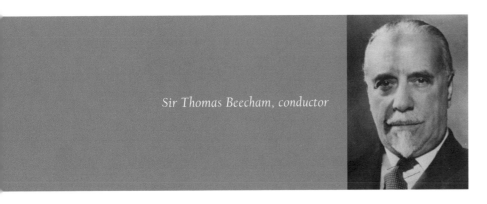

Sir Thomas Beecham, conductor

Composers Samuel Adler and Aaron Copland (right)

Aaron Copland rehearses the Rochester Philharmonic Orchestra (below)

riage counselor as the various romantic entanglements of both assumed awesome proportions.

In 1931 Goossens accepted the post of conductor of the Cincinnati Symphony Orchestra, remaining there until 1946. There he was noted for his "adventurous programs, elegant demeanor on the podium, and public eloquence," according to David Stybr. In 1942 Goossens commissioned a series of ten fanfares from American composers as a patriotic gesture during wartime. The composers included Morton Gould, Howard Hanson, and Virgil Thomson. The most famous of these fanfares, and perhaps the most popular ever composed, was *Fanfare for the Common Man* by Aaron Copland. Eventually, Sir Eugene Goossens became regarded by many as one of the great conductors of the early twentieth century.

Coates and Goossens marked the beginning of the Rochester Philharmonic Orchestra's fascination with British conductors and music directors, a fascination that would continue with Sir Thomas Beecham, Sir Mark Elder, and Christopher Seaman.

When music was played
he lost the austerity and reserve which characterized him
in his daily business life and contacts.

—Eugene Goossens describing Eastman

Finally the Hush Lived Expectant

Paul Horgan's brief "Chapter XIV: Theater Moment" describes the opening minutes of an early Rochester Philharmonic concert. With real persons substituted in brackets for Horgan's fictional ones, here is part of that chapter:

[Goossens] gave his first concert of the season...The circumstance in the [Eastman Theatre] was enlivening, with limousines drawing up, and horns sounding, and the doormen busy until their coat tails whirled and glittered.... There was life in the golden bustle and flutter in the filling auditorium.... The orchestra was seated. The men caressed their instruments, softly testing and correcting the tuning, and the librarians moved around for a final inspection of the music sheets.... [Lucille Bigelow] sat down [at her harp] and ran through her music, and then with her thumb ran over her strings so softly no sound took flight. Then she too settled into the wait. Mr. [Eastman] arrived...and took his place...The subdued murmur went on...and then there was the unanimous hush, as if by signal, and the concertmaster tapped his lectern with his bow. The lights in the auditorium softened slowly...and then, with a preoccupied air, [Goossens] stepped from behind the left proscenium and the orchestra arose to greet him.... He was extraordinary in his smartness and his tempered air of pleasure at the rolling applause. He stopped, put his hand on his heart and bowed from the waist. Then he went on to his dais, and waved his arms to the men, seating them. He had to turn to bow three or four times to quiet the audience. Finally the hush lived expectant. He raised his arms.... The poised bows bit their strings. The cymbals, the brasses, the kettle-drums stated the music. It was a concert of great style and beauty.

Christopher Seaman conducting the Rochester Philharmonic Orchestra on Opening Night, 2009

*P*art II of our story, *The Magic Endures*, begins with this chapter, *Pageantry from a Giant Gazebo*, about the magnificent art, architecture, and furnishings that endure from the earliest days of the Eastman Theatre. Chief among them is the glorious chandelier bursting from its gilded, coffered ceiling and the murals depicting eight categories of music against a landscape featuring Italian hill towns and their craggy suroundings. The next two chapters trace the development of two enduring George Eastman legacies, the Eastman School of Music (ESM) and the Rochester Philharmonic Orchestra (RPO).

PART TWO

The Magic Endures

THE EASTMAN THEATRE AFTER EASTMAN

In a sense he is still there: every mural, marble block, and chandelier is a reminder of his meticulous supervision.

ARCHITECTS OF BEAUTY AND STYLE

In Beaux-Arts design the landscape is an extension of architecture, and the smallest detail is connected to the vision of the whole. The murals, chandelier, sculpture, carvings, and paintings are thus an extension of the architecture of the Eastman Theatre. Behind the scenes, Lawrence Grant White and his hand-picked decorating crew were part of the Dublin or the Cornish art colonies centering on Mount Monadnock in New Hampshire. Among the other artists in those colonies were Charles Platt, Bertram Goodhue, Paul Manship, Barry Faulkner, and Augustus Saint-Gaudens. The Eastman Theatre and School of Music would be White's first major project, and he was determined to make it a showcase success. Larry was the only surviving child of Stanford White, the Gilded Age's most prominent neo-classical architect whose scandalous life and tragic death sometimes hide his enormous talents as draftsman and architect.

The bristling Stanford White's character was in many respects the opposite of fellow architect Charles McKim. He was described by his son, Larry, as "exuberant, restless, a skyrocket of vitality."

During a suggestive chorus song, "I Could Love a Million Girls," at the Madison Square Roof Garden (a building that Stanford White had designed fifteen years previously), Stanford White was shot and killed point blank by Harry Thaw, the jealous millionaire husband of Evelyn Nesbit. White had had a manipulative sexual relationship with this actress and artist's model when she was sixteen (to his forty-seven). The initial reaction was that this was just an elaborate party trick. When it became apparent that White was dead, hysteria ensued. William Randolph Hearst's newspapers sensationalized the murder as the Trial of the Century.

The elder White's energy and output had been gargantuan. He had designed many of the landmarks of New York City and elsewhere, including the palaces for the kind of people we know only through the novels of Edith Wharton. Stanford's son inherited many of these traits. Larry was an amateur musician; he and artist Barry Faulkner discovered they both loved playing duets on the piano, especially Mozart's *Jupiter Symphony*. This soon expanded to two pianos and eight hands and they formed a group called the Octomaniacs. In Faulkner's eyes, White was "a prodigy, a man of astounding energy with many gifts and interests. Besides his passion for music, he was fluent in four languages, wrote a verse translation of *The Divine Comedy*, painted attractive watercolors, and wrote delightful

As entertaining as Larry White found his father's bending the axis to solve an architectural problem, he was not amused when George Eastman insisted on bending the axis of the Eastman Theatre to accommodate its peculiarly shaped lot.

Photographs of Stanford White abound, as do books and movies about his lurid life. Not so

of his son. Eastman had to ask Larry White for a photograph of himself for a booklet being prepared for the theater opening. White replied that he would search for one. Almost ninety

verse with many twists and turns. He was cautious in weighing the character of new acquaintances but once his confidence was established, he became a warm and steadfast friend." Larry White once described his father, contrasting him to his father's partner, the calm, deliberate, shy and cautious scholar, Charles McKim:

years later, a photograph of the younger White is equally hard to find. After his father's murder, Larry White went into hiding with his aggrieved mother, only to emerge thirteen years later when he received the Eastman Theatre commission. In a 1956 interview, shortly before his sudden death, Larry White said, "My college course [at Harvard] was interrupted by my father's death, which was a terrible shock….My relationship to my father was not very close. He was terribly busy." When the interviewer pressed, "What about the effect upon your own life of your father's death? Was there difficulty at Harvard about it?"

> [Stanford] White's character was in many respects the opposite of [Charles] McKim's. He was exuberant, restless, a skyrocket of vitality. He worked at terrific pressure and produced a great many buildings, which are graceful and charming rather than imposing, and often profusely ornamented. He was always striving for new effects, and never hesitated to be architecturally incorrect in order to solve a problem. Once a draughtsman came to him in despair because the axis of a scheme which he had indicated could not be maintained. "Damn it all, bend the axis," was the reply.

"No. No," White responded, "Everybody there was very kind to me but I kept very quiet for that reason during that junior year." His mother, Bessie White, closed the New York house and moved to Cambridge, where she and her son lived quietly. "When I graduated in three years at age nineteen, we folded up and went to Egypt and Greece and Italy." When Larry White attended the École des Beaux-Arts, Bessie followed and took an apartment in Paris, and when he became secretary to the American ambassador in Rome, she took a house there. Although he married in June 1916 and the first of his eight children began to arrive, White does not mention this milestone in his 1956 memoir. As with John D. Rockefeller, Douglas MacArthur, and Franklin Delano Roosevelt, in that era, his mother was always "Darling," while his wife was just "Dear."

Larry White and his future wife, Laura Astor Chanler, were the same age almost to the day, had attended the same dance class, and began dating each other when they were both seventeen. Larry was a callow, handsome, polished youth; his father, Stanford, was not so polished but more bristling with life. Stanford's red hair turned up in Larry's moustache. The two tended to be irritable with each other, Stanford's great-granddaughter Suzannah Lessard recorded in a tell-all memoir, *The Architect of Desire: Beauty and Danger in the Stanford White Family*. Larry himself wrote that even after Laura and the children entered his life, he was very close to his mother and paternal grandmother, indeed "tied to my mother's apron strings from 1906 to 1919." The theater commission coincided with liberation from those apron strings.

Laura and Larry were with Stanford White the day he was shot; indeed, he invited them to go to dinner but Laura had to catch the Lackawanna train to Sweet Briar Farm in Geneseo, New York, where she and her parents and her seven younger siblings lived. According to his granddaughter, Larry White testified at the trial that he had never heard of Evelyn Nesbit. He then never publicly mentioned the subject again except once when he wrote, "On the night of June 25th, 1906, while attending a performance at Madison Square Garden, Stanford White was shot from behind [by] a crazed profligate whose great wealth was used to besmirch his victim's memory during the series of notorious trials that ensued." Privately, Suzannah Lessard writes, Larry spoke of it only once to Laura Chanler, saying, "I suppose that means we can't be married," to which Laura replied, "Don't be silly."

The Theatre as Cathedral to Music

Have you ever wondered why the Eastman Theatre, a movie theater, should have romantic yet classical murals full of allusions to myth and visible mainly from the balcony level, as if they were the stained glass windows in the clerestory of a medieval cathedral? Why is the haloed St. Cecilia at her organ the most important of the murals? Why do White's other Rochester commissions have medieval religious overtones? How much influence did Laura Chanler White have on her husband's designs?

Laura Chanler White's mother, Margaret Terry, known familiarly as Daisy, is written up in *Genesee Valley Women, 1743-1985* by Irene Beale, as well as in her own three memoirs, one of which, *Roman Spring*, became a bestseller. Daisy Terry was born in Rome to painter Luther Terry and Louisa Ward Terry. Her aunt was Julia Ward Howe, with whom she lived intermittently and her friends included Henry Adams, Isabelle Stewart Gardiner, and Edith Wharton. Daisy married her cousin, Winthrop "Wintie" Chanler, whom she described as "a dear well-to-do idler," and together they lived in Washington, D.C.; Geneva, Switzerland; Rome; Paris; New York City; and Newport, Rhode Island; finally settling on Sweet Briar, a summer place in Geneseo, New York, in 1903, upon the invitation of Major William Austin Wadsworth to join the Genesee Valley Hunt.

As the patron of music, musicians, musical instrument makers, singers, composers and poets, St. Cecilia (at left, in a detail from the theater's mural "Sacred Music") is represented by roses and musical instruments, especially lutes, viols, and organs.

The Fountain Court addition to the Memorial Art Gallery of 1926 (below right) is another Lawrence White design with ceiling by Ezra Winter and featured painting by Luca Giordano (1634–1705).

Early on, Daisy Terry converted to Roman Catholicism, which Wintie's sisters and others found scandalous, but it cemented her friendship with Henry Adams, who was newly interested in the French Middle Ages and Chartres. Adams addressed Daisy as "Dear Gentle Saint" and "a sister of the twelfth century," saying that none of his other many women friends had ever heard of the twelfth century.

Daisy and Wintie had eight children: the five girls were raised Roman Catholic, the three boys Episcopalian. Laura, the eldest, was particularly devout. Because "a country place [Sweet Briar] did not seem complete without a chapel," Laura and her mother designed and directed the construction of the Chapel of St. Felicitas overlooking the Genesee Valley. Sixteen-year-old Laura painted a trellis of pomegranates on the apse and grapevines in the sanctuary, and across the face of the apse, she crafted a Latin verse. Sweet Briar Farm was a 600-acre summer retreat. In the fall Daisy would pack up seven children (young John having died), their attendants, a Steinway grand, and a thoroughbred mare. The ménage then sailed to Europe where the younger children went to English schools while Laura studied painting in Paris. The family had high hopes for Laura's success as an artist but instead she married Larry White in 1916 and had eight children of her own.

Because of the theater design and his marriage to a Genesee Valley woman, Larry White had other Rochester commissions. The commission for the 1926 Fountain Court addition to the Memorial Art Gallery developed because patron James Sibley Watson and his stepson James Averell, in whose memory the gallery was given, were members of the Genesee Valley Hunt—as was Larry White. The Fountain Court has a clerestory and Zenitherm "stone" walls in part because White was the architect and in part because gallery director Gertrude Herdle was a medievalist. Through Herdle's influence the Watsons became medievalists, too. More recently the Fountain Court acquired both a 17th century Italian baroque organ and a major religious painting by Luca Giordano—echoing the Giordano in the Eastman Theatre that was once owned by Stanford White.

And then there is the Byzantine Rochester Savings Bank designed by William Kendall and Larry White. White engaged Ezra Winter to make a colorful mosaic that featured a winged "Prosperity" rewarding "Industry" and "Thrift." Taking advantage of the mosaic, the architects adapted the Byzantine style. Located in the part of Rochester that was home to many Eastern European immigrants and next to St. Joseph's Church, the bankers noted that many customers came in to make a deposit, looked around in awe, especially at the mosaic, then crossed themselves and genuflected before Prosperity and her children, Industry and Thrift.

Pageantry from a Giant Gazebo

When noisy and bumptious sixth graders make their annual trek to the Eastman Theatre, they sit awestruck in hushed silence waiting for the program to start. The place is just so imposing, so different from their school auditoriums, that they are cowed into taking in the splendors surrounding them. This is what the theater planners wanted.

Larry White was charged with decorating the theater, inside and out. Among his first tasks was consulting with his chosen muralists and sculptors. One can imagine him telling them that the scheme for the auditorium was that of the audience sitting in a huge elaborate pavilion open to the classical outdoors. These outdoor scenes should depict ensembles of figures creating various types of music against a background of Italian hill towns. Below the arcaded scenes, the Zenitherm walls would look like rusticated stonework.

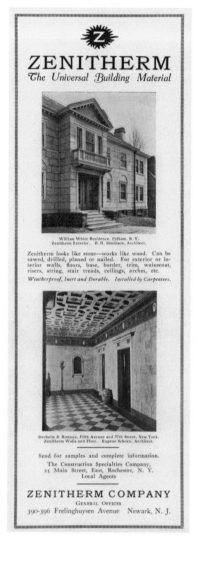

Unlike stone, Zenitherm is a thermal material made from corncobs, warm to the touch and, like cork, absorbent of both sound and moisture. During its days as a movie theater, White himself would design three stage settings for motion pictures, orchestra concerts, and recitals. The ones for orchestra and the movie screen were made to look like scenes in an Italian garden.

With simple changes of curtains or flats, the original Eastman stage as Larry White envisioned it could go from a set for movies accompanied by a theater orchestra to an orchestra-only concert stage or to a stage set for a piano recital.

The steel stage (near right) was designed by George C. Izenour in the early 1970s. It was replaced in 2004.

The 2004 stage of the Eastman Theatre (middle right) continues the arcade theme of the murals and the Zenitherm look of the lower walls, but in plywood. Its main function is to improve the acoustics.

In the 1970s the famous stage designer George C. Izenour designed a new steel stage that resembled an eyelid covered with fish scales, which people remember counting as children. But the stage weighed eleven tons, was heavy and clunky to put up and take down, and terrible for acoustics. In 2004 that failed metal shell was replaced by a plywood one that continues the arcade theme of the murals above and the Zenitherm look below. Mainly, the present stage was designed to improve the acoustics.

A shallow dome similar to the dome of the Pantheon in Rome was designed by White and decorated by Ezra Winter. In place of the Pantheon's oculus open to sky and sun, an enormous chandelier illuminates and dominates the theater auditorium. To enhance the charm of the vast auditorium, the walls are embellished with eight mural paintings located at balcony level. Bas-reliefs above the murals in the form of cherubs and musical instruments were created by sculptor Carl Paul Jennewein. Higher up, the cornice is decorated with arabesque patterns of harps and shields, scrolls, griffins, and winged seahorses.

For circular niches above and guarding the main emergency exits on the orchestra level near each side of the stage, youthful sculptor Leo Friedlander created heroic, double life-sized gilded busts of Ludwig van Beethoven and Johann Sebastian Bach. Bach was not a favorite of Eastman, who compared his music to "sawing wood." Portrait medallions set into the balcony rail and ceiling honor seventeen celebrated composers. Mozart is fifth from the left. The proscenium arch generously ornamented with masks of tragedy and comedy features a shield with the University of Rochester "Я R" legend supported on either side by an unusual winged classical figure holding a torch. Interestingly, patrons in the most expensive seats in the house, the orchestra seats, did not

get the benefit of all of this decoration and had the worst acoustics to boot. The acoustical failures were corrected by the 2004 to 2010 renovations but the murals, chandelier, and glorious ceiling are still most visible from the balcony level.

Ludwig van Beethoven has short tousled hair (above).

Johann Sebastian Bach wears a curly, long-haired wig (left).

Arabesque patterns of harps and shields, scrolls, griffins, and winged seahorses decorate the cornices of the theater (below).

Bas-reliefs (below) above the murals in the form of cherubs and musical instruments were created by the German-born American Art Deco sculptor Carl Paul Jennewein. Jennewein won a Prix de Rome and studied at the American Academy in Rome with Howard Hanson, Barry Faulkner, and Ezra Winter.

The Murals

Eight towering allegorical landscapes seen through enormous architectural openings depict colorful and poetic yesterdays. Educated audiences in the 1920s would have understood the stories of musical and classical mythology seen in the foregrounds. A partial balustrade projects into the auditorium space separating audience from murals. Sketches in color of the murals were planned and drawn by the artists at one inch to the foot then enlarged with the help of assistants and stereopticon projectors. Since neither Barry Faulkner nor Ezra Winter had a studio with ceilings high enough to paint oil on canvas panels that ranged from twenty-one to twenty-eight feet in height, the two artists leased space in the vast attic of Grand Central Terminal. This space provided sufficient altitude to accommodate panels and the length to paint the eight panels side by side. The artists "enclosed [their] studio space with a ten-foot wall of heavy plywood and divided it down the middle with a partition," according to Faulkner's posthumously published memoir, *Sketches from an Artist's Life*. "This partition was valuable, for through it Ezra and I saw how each other's work progressed and kept the panels harmonious in tone and color without discussion or effort."

However, two visits from their ultimate patron left the artists disheartened. On his first visit, Eastman saw the murals "in the chalk" and after the second visit, Faulkner recorded: "Mr. George Eastman's inspection of the murals depressed us. He gazed at them with a heavy eye and made no comment." Perhaps the artists did not know that Eastman was a seventh-grade dropout and may not have understood classical mythology as well as they did. Eastman also sent his friend Frank Babbott of Brooklyn, who had introduced him to McKim, Mead & White in 1902, to check on the progress of the work from time to time.

Mural painting and lunch in the attic of Grand Central Terminal (left)

Barry Faulkner at work on the mural "Pastoral Music" (below)

At least three of the artists—Winter, Faulkner, and Jennewein—trained through scholarships to the American Academy in Rome (established by Larry White's older colleague, Charles McKim); this could partially explain their reliance on classical themes and interpretations. Ezra Winter specialized in architectural ornament and had general supervision over the color schemes and decorations of the entire theater and school, including Kilbourn Hall. Winter was a meticulous craftsman; it is said he painted the Kilbourn Hall ceiling himself. His work in the two theaters soon led to other Rochester commissions. Between 1923 and 1926, he worked on an auditorium (now gone) for the Memorial Art Gallery and the ceiling of its new Fountain Court. He did murals for a bank on State Street and the ceiling and colorful mosaics for the nearby new Rochester Savings Bank on Franklin Street. All three of the artists—Winter, Faulkner, and Jennewein—would go on to do murals and sculpture for Rockefeller Center in the 1930s. In Winter's case, his sweeping three-story canvas lining the Grand Staircase is set against another soaring gilded ceiling and illuminated by twenty-nine-foot-high crystal chandeliers built by E. F. Caldwell, Inc. It was the Caldwell chandeliers that did not arrive in time for the opening of the Eastman Theatre and thus were replaced by lighting fixtures hastily constructed of washtubs. (See anecdote on page 37.)

Contemporaries of Winter and Faulkner said that the artists used the various architects, workmen, acousticians, and theater staff members as models for the fictionalized mythical or Renaissance figures. Concertgoers of earlier eras could identify those models. Unfortunately, no one has left a key to these presumed portraits.

Painted during the full flush of early twentieth century romanticism, Ezra Winter's four colorful paintings (below) on the left wall of the Eastman Theatre looking toward the stage represent (left to right) sylvan, martial, lyric, and festival music.

On the opposite wall, paintings by Barry Faulkner (below, left to right) symbolize sacred, hunting, pastoral, and dramatic music. Faulkner, who studied with Abbott Thayer and George de Forest Brush, would specialize in historical murals: he is perhaps best known for his murals for Rockefeller Center and of the Declaration of Independence and The Constitution for the National Archives.

SYLVAN MUSIC

Next to the seats in the loges, Ezra Winter portrayed his conception of "Sylvan Music." Three minstrels play to the lithe gyrations of a dancing girl. Trees and waterfalls form the background with flocks of birds on the wing, suggesting freedom of movement in the outdoors. The green foliage establishes the predominant color and is accented by the warm reds and yellows in the picturesque dress of the minstrels and dancing girl in the foreground.

MARTIAL MUSIC

In the foreground of Winter's "Martial Music," a heroic group of three horsemen with trumpets carrying a scarlet banner is led by a bagpiper, a drummer boy and two dogs, the latter symbolizing the "dogs of war." The landscape also suggests the severe hardness of military life and the devastations of war. (The painting was done a few years after the carnage of World War I.) A mountain crag, bleak and austere, forms the distant background, while broken trees and the barrenness and coldness of the rocks, many of them torn asunder, in the middle background imply spiritual struggles. The boldness of design and execution and the predominant colors of black and scarlet breathe a spirit of militarism and an atmosphere of martial combat.

As for the dogs of war, the reference is Shakespearean. (The dogs in a sense personify—or "caninify"—war.) "Caesar's spirit, raging for revenge…come hot from hell, Shall in these confines with a monarch's voice Cry 'Havoc', and let slip the dogs of war, that this foul deed shall smell above the earth with carrion men, groaning burial." Thus spake Shakespeare's Mark Antony, predicting that savage havoc will be visited on the conspirators for the death of Julius Caesar.

LYRIC MUSIC

Winter portrays "Lyric Music" as romantic, poetic and suggestive of Shakespeare. A castle in the distance conveys an atmosphere of romance as pictured in the dreams of romantic youth. The broken masonry in the middle distance typifies the dramatic aspect of lyric drama. The four figures in the foreground are garbed in Florentine and Venetian dress. A medieval musician plays the lute while three graceful, allegorical female figures represent Soprano, Mezzo, and Contralto.

Festival Music

"Festival Music" is Winter's signature scene, with the master of ceremonies right next to the theater stage holding a ceremonial staff topped by a lyre. Festooned musicians with garlands flank him while young pages in the foreground express the good looks and high spirits of youth. (Note the similarity in the detail of design in the coffers of this arch and those of the Eastman Theatre chandelier dome.) Three trumpeters at the foot of the great classical arch represent the ceremonial aspects. Suspended from that arch is the magnificent Renaissance lamp still extant in Pisa that Winter remembered from his student days in Italy.

SACRED MUSIC

"Sacred Music," the 28-foot high mural under the arch next to the stage, is Barry Faulkner's signature scene. We see a slender, haloed St. Cecilia seated at her organ, her crimson lining trailing below the organ bench, while above float the angelic twin spirits of music. The real Cecilia was a cultivated young woman who lived in the second century. As daughter of a Roman patrician, Cecilia was arranged to be married against her will to a non-Christian named Valerian. She convinced him to respect her virginity, converted him to Christianity, and then converted his brother. The two men were caught burying the bodies of martyred Christians and, along with Cecilia, were arrested and executed. Cecilia's musical fame rests on a passing notice in her legend that she praised God, singing to him as she lay dying a martyr's death in the boiling water of her own bath. As the patron of music, musicians, musical instrument makers, singers, composers and poets, St. Cecilia is represented by roses and musical instruments, especially lutes, viols, and organs.

HUNTING MUSIC

Faulkner continues the concept of landscape as an extension of architecture in his next mural, "Hunting Music." Three trumpeters abreast sound their triumphant return upon slender, looped horns seen against the misty background of a walled city with towers, domes and pale walls rising into the hills where the mystery of unseen forces abides. The trumpeters are followed by an archer with a white dog and preceded by a boy carrying a dead fowl.

Pastoral Music

Is that Apollo, god of music, poetry, and oracles atop the canopy in Faulkner's mural "Pastoral Music"? "A faun youth pipes to a canopy covered maiden. Another half-clad maiden dances and gaily clashes her cymbals while a woman servant watches from behind the canopy," said the 1922 newspapers. In mythology, fauns and the Roman god Faunus, goat-people all, are similar to the Greek god Pan. Pan was the god of shepherds and flocks, of mountain wilds, hunting and rustic music. He wandered the hills and mountains of Arcadia playing his pan-pipes and chasing nymphs, who commonly fled from his advances. One nymph was transformed into a clump of reeds out of which the god crafted his famous pan-pipes. His unseen presence aroused feelings of panic in men passing through the remote, wild and lonely places.

Dramatic Music

Located at the south end of the loges seats, Barry Faulkner painted "Dramatic Music," a mural depicting masks of comedy and tragedy, set in a woodland scene with various shades of leaves. An erect buffoon with a shepherd's crook carries the comedy mask while a damsel holding the tragedy mask beckons him on. In the foreground, a grotesque Silenus, minor woodland deity of ancient Greek mythology and companion of Dionysius, is astride his mule. But who is the ugly gnome with wings standing in a Greek temple in the crotch of the gnarled tree?

The chandelier is fourteen feet in diameter, thirty-five feet tall, weighs approximately 5000 pounds (2 1/2 tons), has 546 visible and 670 concealed lights, and has 298 strings of glass containing 20,000 individual pieces of crystal going from the circle to the top.

*C*HANDELIER

The chandelier is fourteen feet in diameter, thirty-five feet tall, weighs approximately 5000 pounds (2 1/2 tons), has 546 visible and 670 concealed lights, and has 298 strings of glass containing 20,000 individual pieces of crystal going from the circle to the top. It never leaves Kodak Hall but every two or three years, usually in August, it is lowered to the main floor for cleaning and bulb replacement. Cleaning takes about three days. Legend has it that the chain was reinforced after the Lon Chaney motion picture *Phantom of the Opera* was released in 1929. While rumored to have done so, it has never fallen.

In 1954 a four-ton section of the ceiling fell on empty seats in the theater as Dr. Herman Genhart rehearsed the *Bach Magnificat* with the Eastman School Orchestra and Chorus. Portions of the chandelier were damaged in this massive drop. The chandelier itself survived although it had to be lowered and repaired while the ceiling was reconstructed. During the 1970s Kodak renovation, 546 clear glass bulbs replaced frosted bulbs, and the original teardrop at the base—lost for twenty years in a backstage workroom—was rediscovered and reinstalled. When the first phase of the latest Eastman Theatre renovation began in 2004, a dust curtain between stage and auditorium was hung but the chandelier still got dirty. The second phase of the renovation began with the lowering of the chandelier on 2 July 2008. To protect it during the work, it was covered in plastic then uncovered and raised until the summer of 2009.

CHERUBIC FOUNTAIN AND ALLEGORICAL PAINTING

Rounding out the wealth of artistic treasures gathered together in this temple to great music are a decorative fountain showing a cherub toying with a dolphin and an allegorical late Baroque painting. Note that architect Lawrence White chose to treat the theater as a music hall rather than a movie palace. The painting is by Luca Giordano "whose voluptuous feminine figures aroused a good deal of controversy," wrote Arthur May, university historian. May stated further that the Giordano "was acquired from the recently dismantled residence of a New York City banker." Actually, according to Roger Butterfield, it came from the estate of Stanford White. When Stanford and Bessie White were first married and lived on rural Long Island, a neighbor, the Rev. Timothy O'Slap, noticed than Stanford had installed "a low and curious seat surrounded by classical statues absolutely devoid of all clothing." The sight caused the reverend to "flee in confusion," a reaction similar to that which greeted son Larry White's use of the Giordano in the balcony of the Eastman Theatre.

The fountain is a copy of one by Giovanni de Bologna (1558-1617) of Florence and probably another architectural fragment or copy from the vast storehouses originally assembled by Stanford White. The elder White took trips to Europe to scour for antiquities for his wealthy clients. It was said that if Stanford White could not procure the right antiques for his interiors, he would sketch, say, a neo-Georgian standing electrolier or a Renaissance library table, and have them made as a perfect copy of some (usually) Italian original. Larry White used a copy of a fountain in the Palazzo Vecchio in Florence for the 1926 Fountain Court of the Memorial Art Gallery. (This, despite the preference by Dr. James Sibley Watson Jr, half brother of James Averell, in whose memory the gallery was given, for a gilded bronze sculpture by Gaston Lachaise for that addition.)

"Psyche and Cupid," a Greek and Roman progenitor tale related to later stories of "Cinderella," "Beauty and the Beast," and "Pandora's Box," is a rare fairytale handed down from antiquity. Perhaps that was why Larry White chose an ensemble of French scenic wallpapers (twelve motifs) in grisailles (shades of gray) portraying this timeless story from the classical era for the lobby and mezzanine. The myth obtained its unmistakable character through the Roman writer Apuleius and has been a source of fascination for painters and sculptors throughout the ages. The story, based on a novel by Jean de la Fontaine, was revived during the nineteenth century because it had all the qualities sought during the romantic period: apparent harmony troubled by ominous signs, emotions lurching from heights of ecstasy to the depths of despair, with the desired result achieved through higher understanding.

Frenchman Louis Lafitte, who won the Premier Prix de Rome in 1791, and Merry-Joseph Blondel designed the original wallpaper, 1814-1816, for Napoleon. It was first printed by hand in a Paris atelier in 1816, using some 1,450 blocks. News of the design spread, and it quickly became popular. It was reprinted frequently—in brown and later in green tones for the interiors of palaces in France and Germany and printed onto continuous paper rolls for the first time around 1830. The twelve large-scale wallpaper scenes that Lawrence White chose for the Eastman Theatre were also probably created around that date.

Psyche, third and youngest daughter of the king and queen of Sicily (in the Roman version) was so beautiful that Venus found her own altars deserted. Shaking her ambrosial locks with indignation, Venus called her mischievous winged son, Cupid, to "infuse into the bosom of that haughty girl a passion for some low, mean, unworthy being." Cupid filled two amber vases, one

Six of the twelve French scenic wallpaper panels depicting the story of Psyche and Cupid (shown here in Eastman Theatre's Oval Lobby in 1993), have been reinstalled in the lobby, four line the passageway to the new wing, and two are on display in the theater's mezzanine.

Psyche at the Bath

Psyche Abandoned

Psyche Sheltered by a Fisherman

Although the story is commonly known as "Cupid and Psyche," the details pictured on these pages are from the French scenic wallpaper entitled "Psyche and Cupid" by Dufour.

of sweet waters, the other of bitter, and suspending them from his quiver, hastened to the chamber of the sleeping Psyche. He shed a few bitter drops over her lips and touched her side with the point of his arrow. At the touch she awoke, which so startled the invisible Cupid that he poured the balmy drops of joy over all her silken ringlets.

Psyche's charms procured flattery in abundance, but failed to end in marriage. Her two elder sisters of moderate charms had long been married. Her parents, afraid that they had incurred the anger of the gods, consulted the oracle of Apollo and heard, "The virgin is destined to be the bride of no mortal lover. Her future husband awaits her on the top of the mountain. He is a monster whom neither gods nor men can resist." This dreadful decree dismayed her parents. But Psyche said, "Lead me to that rock to which my unhappy fate has destined me." When Psyche stood on the mountain ridge, the gentle west wind, Zephyr, carried her to a wondrous country where she awoke to a magnificent palace with golden pillars, carvings, and paintings. A disembodied voice spoke, "Sovereign lady, all that you see is yours. Repose on your bed of down then repair to the bath. Supper awaits when it pleases you." A table presented itself covered with the greatest delicacies and most nectarous wines. Psyche's ears feasted on music

from invisible performers: one sang, another played on the lute, and all closed in the wonderful harmony of a full chorus. Her destined husband came only in darkness and fled before dawn, but he was full of love. She begged him to let her behold him, but he would ask, "Why? Have you doubt of my love? Have you wishes ungratified? If you saw me, perhaps you would fear me, perhaps adore me, but all I ask of you is to love me."

This quieted Psyche until the novelty wore off. One night she drew from Cupid an unwilling consent that she should see her elder sisters. The obedient Zephyr brought her down to the sisters' valley where Psyche then led them to her golden palace. This caused much envy, and the sisters made her confess that she had never seen him. They filled her with dark suspicions of the direful and tremendous monster the oracle predicted who nourishes for a while but by and by devours. They advised her to take a lamp and sharp knife to her sleeping husband and cut off the monster's head. Psyche resisted until curiosity overwhelmed. When Cupid had fallen asleep, she beheld not a hideous monster, but the most beautiful of the gods, with golden ringlets wandering over his snowy neck and crimson cheek and two dewy white wings with tender shining feathers. As she leaned, a drop of burning oil fell on Cupid's shoulder. Startled, he opened his eyes and speechless, spread his wings and flew out of the window. In trying to follow him, Psyche fell to the ground.

Cupid, seeing her in the dust, stopped his flight for an instant. "Oh foolish Psyche, is this how you repay my love? After I disobeyed my mother's commands and made you my wife, will you cut off my head? Return to your sisters, whose advice you prefer. I inflict no punishment except to leave you forever. Love cannot live with suspicion." As he flew away, palace and gardens vanished. Psyche then wandered day and night in search of Cupid. Entering a magnificent temple, she saw heaps of corn scattered about with ears of barley, sickles, and rakes. Psyche put an end to this unseemly confusion by separating and sorting everything. The holy Ceres, whose temple it was, then spoke: "Oh Psyche, truly worthy of our pity, I cannot shield you from Venus, but you can allay her displeasure. Voluntarily surrender yourself and try by modesty and submission to win her forgiveness." Psyche went to the temple of Venus. "Most undutiful of servants," said the angry goddess, "do you really remember your mistress? Or have you come to see your husband, laid up with the wound you gave him? You are so disagreeable that you can only merit your lover by dint of industry and diligence. I will make trial of your housewifery." She ordered Psyche to sort the pigeon food of her temple—wheat, barley, millet, vetches, etc.—by separating the grains and getting it done before evening. Psyche sat stupid and silent before the enormous heap until Cupid stirred up a little ant. Soon, hosts of six-legged creatures approached and grain by grain separated the pile, each kind to its parcel. As twilight approached Venus returned and exclaimed, "This is no work of yours, wicked one, but his, whom to his misfortune you have enticed." She threw Psyche a piece of black bread for her supper and left. During the next days, Venus concocted ever more difficult orders, including reaching the realms of Pluto and returning. Psyche obediently did her best with the help of invisible, compassionate gods but Venus always grumbled. Once, carrying a box of divine beauty to Venus, Psyche peeked into the receptacle. Finding instead an infernal Stygian sleep, which took possession of her, Psyche became a corpse without sense or motion.

Cupid, recovered from his wound, and unable to bear the absence of his beloved, slipped through the smallest crack of the window and flew to her. Gathering up the sleep from her body, he closed it again in the box and waked Psyche with a light touch of one of his arrows. "Again," said he, "you have almost perished by curiosity. But now perform exactly the task imposed on you by my mother, and I will take care of the rest."

Swift as lightning, Cupid presented himself before Jupiter, who lent a favoring ear and pleaded the lovers' cause so earnestly with Venus that he won her consent. Jupiter then sent Mercury to bring Psyche up to the heavenly assembly, and when she arrived, handed her a cup of ambrosia, saying, "Drink this, Psyche, and be immortal; nor shall Cupid ever break away from the knot in which he is tied, but these nuptials shall be perpetual." Thus Psyche became at last united with Cupid and in due time they had a daughter named Pleasure (Voluptus), although the poet John Milton says they had twins—Youth and Joy.

Psyche Going to Hades

Psyche Returning from Hades

The Wedding of Psyche and Cupid

CHARLOTTE

Charlotte Whitney Allen's 1936 Ford Cunningham was regularly parked by the entrance to the theater well into the 1950s and '60s. It was even said that the concert could not begin until she had sashayed to her seat. One of the grand dames of Rochester, she regularly held salons at her home on Oliver Street off East Avenue.

Charlotte's good friend Kathleen McEnery (Cunningham) painted the portrait that hangs in the Mezzanine Lounge. McEnery, a student of Robert Henri and an exhibitor (of nudes) in the notorious 1913 Armory show in New York City, moved to Rochester after marrying Francis Cunningham, an executive in the family hearse, carriage and automobile business. Cunningham shared his wife's interest in art and music and became chairman of the board of the David Hochstein Memorial Music School, now the Hochstein School of Music and Dance.

Legend has it that Charlotte founded the famous Corner Club in a building near the theater owned by the Hawley Ward family. (Mrs. Ward was an actress and Charlotte's closest friend.) It happened after Charlotte lit a cigarette while lunching at her mother's Century Club and was told that smoking was not allowed. "Then I shall start my own club," said Charlotte. And she did.

NETTA

Mrs. Robert (Netta) Ranlet, for whom the Eastman-Ranlet Concert series is named, was the founder of the Women's Committee of the Civic Music Association—now the Rochester Philharmonic League. In describing her friend George Eastman, Netta told interviewers that he believed that all sorts of people should gather together and get to know one

another. He also believed that music, like silent films, was a universal language. Thus, "all sorts of people" received invitations to his Sunday musicales, with the guest list changing and expanding weekly. His theater was planned to appeal to "all sorts of people." Eastman quietly enjoyed the sight of the group spirit in action whether in his home or his reserved chair in the mezzanine of the Eastman Theatre, which he could reach by a special door, long since plastered over, from the subscribers staircase in the Eastman School of Music.

"His best went into everything from building the Eastman Theatre to lighting a cigarette," Netta explained. Operation smoking began with removing the leather container from his pocket, then unfastening the flap, selecting a cigarette and neatly securing it in the holder, returning the pack to his pocket, and finally lighting the cigarette and carefully disposing of the match. Onlookers were held spellbound, remembering it in vivid detail. This preoccupation with details carried over. When showing Netta around the unfinished theater, Eastman came upon a small trowel used in sculpting the ornate ceiling. "Look how they have one just the right size," he exclaimed delightedly. "It fits exactly where it is to go."

Clayla

Mrs. F. Hawley (Clayla) Ward, a past president of the Women's Committee of the Civic Music Association, was present at the Eastman Theatre on opening night and most nights thereafter until her death in 1973. She was usually accompanied by music critic A. J. Warner II in white tie and tails; the glittering pair stopped many times to greet other concert-goers as they glided down the aisle.

Clayla recalled opening night: "Throngs of people in high fashion...filled the seats....The men wore spanking white shirts and full dress suits. The orchestra players were decked out in uniforms of a marching band."

Clara Louise (Clayla) Werner and Charlotte Whitney called each other "Charlie" and "Chuck" as childhood pals, traveled throughout Europe and the Near East together when slightly older, and matured into philanthropists. Their friend James Rieger, University of Rochester professor of English, has written: "Both girls grew into ladies who transcended a class no longer extant. They fostered music and art, promoted tolerance, and catalyzed good talk in a town that must have disheartened less robust natures."

At one Rochester Philharmonic Orchestra benefit concert, Clayla took part in a parody of modern music, "playing" a floor polisher. "Make it a small machine, Dah-ling," she instructed the stage manager. "I've never worked in my life." Actually, no

Opening Night at the Eastman Theatre

By Mrs. F. Hawley Ward

The night the Eastman Theatre opened was a gala, gala occasion. It also was a tremendous tribute to the man whose dreams had created it.

I remember the opening well because it was the first time my husband, Hawley, and I had come back to Rochester from Canandaigua, where we had lived all that summer.

We had been married earlier that year, in February 1922, and had spent the winter in Nassau. When we arrived back in the states, we went to Canandaigua where his family had a summer home. The opening of the Eastman was the first occasion we'd had to return to Rochester.

I had kept track of the theater's construction and now was thrilled to finally see throngs of people in high fashion fill its seats.

Flags were flying outside from the marquee—an Eastman Theatre flag and an American flag.

Car after car pulled up to a ous. The orchestra players were dressed in uniforms, like a marching band, and looked very exquisite.

Then there was a dance number, the opera and the movie, "The Prisoner of Zenda."

The audience loved all of it. It was very well received.

I knew George Eastman very well. He was good friends with my father and I discovered he also liked me because I had what he called "common sense."

used constantly after its opening in September. There were daily matinees attended regularly by children and their mothers. Husbands would stop in at the theater on their way home from work.

It also became the habit after evening performances for my husband and I to invite performers back to our home a block away for some refreshments and conversation.

Conductors like Arthur Alexander, Eugene Goossens and Albert Coates and his wife, Madeline, from England, graced our halls several times. It was a wonderful time to be living.

There was never a "forced march" down to the Eastman Theatre. The people came the first time for Mr. Eastman. Then they began coming for themselves.

No opening would be complete without the presence of one of Rochester's most honored women, Mrs. F. Hawley Ward, or "Clayla"

one worked harder for the RPO than Clayla, albeit in a volunteer capacity. Bejeweled, perfumed, and elegantly dressed, Clayla addressed one and all as "Dah-ling" in a throaty contralto and knew every Rochester cab driver. Once, when she was mugged and robbed in her home near the Eastman Theatre and urged to move to a "safer" neighborhood, she refused, protesting, "I was here first."

Clayla was one of the three beautiful daughters of Judge William Werner. Another was Caroline (Kyrie) Werner Gannett, who had married the founder of the Gannett newspaper chain. Today, Juliana Athayde, concertmaster of the RPO, occupies the Caroline W. Gannett and Clayla Ward chair, funded in perpetuity.

On 15 September 1924, Howard Hanson— lanky, blond, six weeks shy of his twenty-eighth birthday, but supremely confident in his own abilities to do almost anything in the music line —arrived permanently in Rochester.

Benito from Wahoo

Eastman School historian Vincent Lenti ends his first volume of the school's history by noting that Howard Hanson was only thirty-five at the time of George Eastman's death. He had been director of the Eastman School for eight years and had thirty-two more to serve as director, plus seventeen more of an influential retirement. When he arrived in Rochester, it was Mr. Eastman's school, Lenti writes. When he retired, it was Mr. Hanson's.

After a January 1924 grilling of Howard Hanson (above) by Rush Rhees and George Eastman, Eastman floated a question. Did Hanson's goatee hide a weak chin? At the American Academy in Rome, composer Randall Thompson could attest that Hanson was in no way weak: "My god," said Thompson. "Howard is president of the student body. We call him 'Benito.'"

In 1923, with Klingenberg's fate decided, Eastman and Rhees went looking first for "an American...or at least a man of English speech...who could make our school a factor in the development of American music without running into the danger of narrow provincialism." Second, they wanted "a man whose education was general as well as musical," and third "a man with administrative experience in a school of music associated with a college of arts and science." Fourth, they looked for "a man of wide general musical interest rather than a man prominent for virtuosity in one branch of music,"...and fifth they wanted "a man of high character as well as tact in dealing with other men, and power to lead both colleagues and students."

Albert Coates, Eastman's conductor and music advisor in 1924, along with Walter Damrosch, conductor for the New York Symphony, met a young American composer/conductor at the American Academy in Rome. Coates and Damrosch both invited the twenty-seven-year old Howard Hanson from Wahoo, Nebraska, to conduct his new *Nordic Symphony* with the Rochester and New York orchestras respectively.

Earlier, Hanson was invited to Eastman's home to meet Rhees and Eastman. The young composer found himself being grilled by the articulate sixty-three-year old college president and the taciturn seventy-year-old industrialist. Hanson took "an instant liking" to Eastman, finding him "reserved and businesslike." Behind the reserve he detected

Howard Hanson over the years

"inner warmth." Rhees did most of the questioning, but Eastman's queries were "models of clarity and incisiveness," and his "ability to search out the heart of a problem with a minimum of words was both impressive and a little frightening."

Hanson agreed to write a multi-page brief on his opinion of the place of a professional music school in a university. Returning to his beloved Rome, he soon received a letter from Rhees offering him the directorship of the Eastman School of Music.

Hanson's Roman colleagues tried to dissuade him, telling him it would cripple his composing, but Hanson decided that he "had to have a job anyway, so I thought I might as well try my hand at this new school." He brought along his invalid Swedish-immigrant parents, with whom he would live until his marriage in 1946. It was the beginning of a remarkable association between a young man and a young school that would bring worldwide distinction to them both.

Hanson emerged as "benevolent dictator" (as he called himself) of the new school. As with George Whipple, who became the founding dean of the new medical school in 1921, Hanson set the tone for subsequent development of the music school. Long after George Eastman and Rush Rhees were gone, the extended shadows of pioneers Hanson and Whipple remained. The school's excellent financial position following Eastman's death in 1932 enabled it to contribute $100,000 per year toward the survival of the Rochester Philharmonic Orchestra during the troubled years of the Great Depression.

Hanson wrote the scores to Merry Mount *and his symphonies after midnight with pen and ink on music-staff paper.*

The students called him Uncle Howard; he knew all their backgrounds, called each by name, and heard every exam himself. He prided himself on being a teaching dean. He created the crackerjack student orchestra, the Eastman Philharmonia, which played regularly in the Eastman Theatre and on occasion in Carnegie Hall.

Unlike his predecessor, Hanson fell into line with Eastman's pet idea of the movie theater supporting the Eastman Theatre concerts. "Mr. Klingenberg was so antagonistic to the whole theatre enterprise that we were not able to get his cooperation, but with Dr. Hanson it is entirely different," Eastman wrote Eric Clarke, theater manager. Hanson understood Eastman: "He was essentially a simple man, but there were complexities, and severity was the armor of his shyness."

Hanson's special province was American contemporary music. And so to the horror of many traditionalists, the new music crept in. In 1931 Hanson initiated the annual Festival of American Music, which he conducted for forty years, and when he died in 1981, Donal Henahan observed in *The New York Times* that

he had made Rochester "a boom town for American music." The festival introduced works by Roy Harris, Aaron Copland, Russell Bennett, Eastman graduate David Diamond, Bernard Rogers, Randall Thompson, and Wallingford Riegger. Hanson probably sacrificed his composing career in fulfilling his administrative function, but he still won the Pulitzer Prize for his *Symphony No. 4, Op. 34.*

Eastman met with the composers who brought new works to Rochester to be performed at the theater or at Eastman's home. Eastman looked at his commitment to encourage young American composers as a long-term investment, much like the Research Laboratories at Kodak. When one impatient critic carped that a Beethoven had not yet been produced, Eastman retorted, "If we produce one American composer approaching Beethoven in fifty years, I'll think my money is well spent."

Like Eastman, Hanson was a born administrator. Hanson acknowledged that he had "a bad case of hero worship for Mr. Eastman. The picture I have of him is almost a father type," he said in 1972. (Eastman returned the compliment: Hanson was exactly what Eastman would have wanted in a son, Marian Gleason said.) Eastman "was wonderful to work with....if he trusted someone to do a job, he allowed him to go his own way.... And he had a marvelous sense of humor.... Out of these consultations grew a friendship which will always be for me the most important experience of my life," Hanson wrote in 1939.

As Eastman's health and strength began to ebb, his daily visits to school and theater turned into weekly and then monthly visits. Finally he came no more. On 4 March 1932, he turned in his key to the Swan Street garage and on the night of 13 March 1932 he sat in front of the dying fireplace embers at home with Harold Gleason. "Don't let anything happen to the school, Harold," he said before retiring. The next day he died of a self-inflicted gunshot wound.

A Light
Burns Out...

Light Over Eastman Portrait Burns Out At Hour of Death

The light, for years illuminiating the portraait of George Eastman in the second corridor of the Eastman School of Music, burned out at noon yesterday.

Telephoning for quick replacement of that light, the school janitor heard the news of Mr. Eastman's death.

Coincidence? The janitor, who saw the light burning just a few minutes before he saw it burned out and heard the news of the death, is wondering.

12:50 PM 14 MARCH 1932

The upstairs corridor of the Eastman School of Music adjoining the subscribers staircase and entrance to the mezzanine was planned as an art promenade. Here music patrons could promenade during intermissions and enjoy changing exhibitions chosen by George Eastman and George Herdle, director of the Memorial Art Gallery. When friends urged Eastman to have his portrait painted to hang here, he countered with "Would it not satisfy your portrait aspirations if I should be sculpt'd heroic size for one of the figures on the roof, with a camera in one hand and a horn in the other?" Nevertheless, he did engage the artist Louis Betts for a three-quarter-length portrait and chose as a placeholder that hung during opening week of the theater a Betts portrait of Mrs. Howard Young. So fond of this portrait was Eastman that he urged his beautiful neighbor Isabelle Bonbright to have her portrait painted by Betts in this society portrait style. When *The New York Times Magazine* did a story on Eastman's "new adventure" in building the Eastman Theatre and School of Music, the Betts portrait, not surprisingly, was used to illustrate it. The surprise came at the hour of Eastman's death when a janitor saw the light over the portrait burning one moment, heard of the death, and almost immediately noticed that the light was gone.

ROCHESTER DEMOCRAT AND CHRONICLE, SUNDAY.

Art promenade between Eastman Theater and School of Music. To be open to attendants at weekly concerts in theatre.

To my friends My work is done why wait?

GE

The lion in winter: Howard Hanson at the rehearsal of Merry Mount in 1971 as part of Opera Under the Stars in Highland Park (left)

A scene from the 1934 production of Merry Mount that was performed by the Metropolitan Opera Company in New York and in the Eastman Theatre (below right)

MERRY MOUNT: AN IMPORTANT OPERA COMMISSION

In the 1930s the Metropolitan Opera commissioned Howard Hanson to write an opera dedicated to George Eastman (who knew this before his death) and starring Lawrence Tibbett and Gladys Swarthout. *Merry Mount* opened in New York in February 1934 and received fifty curtain calls. Ruth Watanabe of the Sibley Library reviewed this powerful musical drama of the conflict between Puritanism and Cavalierism in the seventeenth century as "one of the comparatively few American productions of monumental scale to be mounted at the Met." She described it as "an interpretation of the conflict of darkness with light, evil with good, chaos and destruction with law and order.... Massacre and incineration crowning tragedy is the only resolution possible. The work ends in a mighty Amen at the moment of the holocaust."

The Eastman Theatre performance by the Met cast followed in April 1934. A second Eastman Theatre production was mounted in 1955 as part of Hanson's Festival of American Music series and yet another in the 1970s in Highland Bowl as part of Opera Under the Stars.

Ruth Watanabe (1916-2005) was the librarian of the Eastman School of Music's Sibley Music Library for nearly four decades.

Librettist and critic Richard L. Stokes wrote the dramatic poem based on the Nathaniel Hawthorne story "The Maypole of Merry Mount." The story featured Thomas Morton, renegade founder of the settlement at Mount Wollaston (now Quincy, Massachusetts) who

scandalously erected a maypole and caused the Puritans no end of consternation. Leonard W. Treash, head of the opera department at the Eastman School of Music, 1947-1976, directed the full-scale production. The choruses represented Puritans, Cavaliers, Demons, and Courtesans.

CENTENNIAL ODE: A YEAR-LONG CELEBRATION

In 1950 the theater played host to the University of Rochester celebrating its centennial as well as the semi-centennial of the admission of women undergraduates, and a quarter century since the beginning of medical instruction. It also marked the retirement of the university's fourth president, Alan Valentine. Beginning with an all-university student convocation in October 1949, Professor Emeritus John R. Slater sketched the high points in the evolution of the university, reminding the audience that it had been a university in an exact sense for only a little while; yet no apologies for its comparative youth were in order. "The University closes no door to ambition," he said, "sets no age when minds cease to grow...."

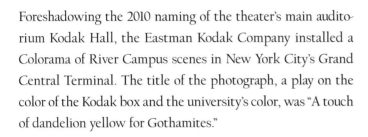

Foreshadowing the 2010 naming of the theater's main auditorium Kodak Hall, the Eastman Kodak Company installed a Colorama of River Campus scenes in New York City's Grand Central Terminal. The title of the photograph, a play on the color of the Kodak box and the university's color, was "A touch of dandelion yellow for Gothamites."

The main celebration was the Alumni-Alumnae Centennial Convocation at the theater on Saturday evening, 10 June 1950 when a capacity audience heard the *Centennial Ode.* Howard Hanson composed and arranged the music; John R. Slater prepared the narrative; Leonard W. Treash performed as narrator. Participating, too, were the Eastman School Chorus of 200 voices and the Eastman School Senior Symphony Orchestra, Hanson conducting.

The *Ode* remembered times past, the progress of the university, and pointed to the challenge of the future— "...of promises fulfilled; of promises still unfulfilled, awaiting wider vision, stronger will"—all attuned to the motto "Meliora." Symbols of university history and the benefactions of George Eastman were evoked.

Hanson's music drew upon Erie Canal chanteys, Walt Whitman's "Drum Taps," and "The Battle Hymn of the Republic." To the audience, the *Ode* brought a tremendous emotional upsurge, university historian Arthur May recorded. The *Ode,* commented a Rochester editor, is as "ageless as a Greek chorus"; for the inspiration and edification of posterity it was placed on a long-playing record.

At graduation rites on June 12, President Alan Valentine delivered his valedictory message, "Time and the University," to the largest graduating class ever. He appealed to the university to combat excessive materialism and the decline in taste, private manners, and public morals. Institutions of higher learning were

sharply reproached for failing "to meet their intellectual and moral challenge"; it was their solemn duty to weave into the lives of their sons and daughters "idealism, truth, and the courage to assert them." Freedom, Valentine concluded, was inseparable from responsibility.

Festivals of American Music

In 1924 Hanson proposed a program that Vincent Lenti wrote "would have long-term implications for the school's strong commitment towards the encouragement of American music." Hanson invited American composers to submit new compositions. Those selected would be played by a professional orchestra and reviewed by professional visiting critics. Aaron Copland scores were among those played by the Rochester Philharmonic Orchestra. The series expanded into the Festival of American Music in 1931. By 1971 the works of more than five hundred composers had been performed in Rochester, mostly at American Composers' concerts and during the Festivals of American Music. Each festival presented a variety of music, which might include opera, ballet, choral works, chamber works and orchestral compositions.

Hanson's inclusion of American works in symphony concerts and NBC radio broadcasts during the 1930s and 1940s helped to create a large audience for contemporary works by American composers. He was justly called the "dean of American composers" and became a spokesman for music in America. Recognition of his contribution to American life and culture included thirty-four honorary doctorates, election into the most prestigious national and international organizations, and buildings named in his honor. The small town of Wahoo still boasts of its famous musician on a large road sign.

John BECK, *percussionist*

Donald HUNSBERGER, *conductor*
Wynton MARSALIS, *trumpeter*

Emory ("The Chief") REMINGTON, *trombonist*

PARADE *of* MASTERS

The Theater as Concert Hall for Large Ensembles...

EASTMAN WIND ENSEMBLE

The wind ensemble (left, with Donald Hunsberger conducting) was invented at Eastman in 1952 by Frederick Fennell (below), who chose percussion as his primary instrument at the age of seven as drummer in the fife-and-drum corps at the family's encampment. As a student in the 1930s, Fennell (the first to be awarded a degree in percussion performance) organized the first University of Rochester marching band for the football team and held indoor concerts with the band after the football season for ten years. In 2010 the Eastman School had more than 27 school-sponsored, independent, or student/faculty ensembles. Eastman produces more than 700 concerts each year.

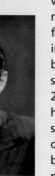

JAZZ ENSEMBLES

Howard Hanson had little use for jazz; so the inclusion of "The Jazz Idiom" featuring the Jazz Quartet led by John Lewis and the Eastman Wind Ensemble directed by Frederick Fennell in the American Festival of 1962 represented a radical departure. Electronic music with commentary by Wayne Barlow followed in 1964, the final festival of Hanson's forty-year tenure, and grew thereafter under director Walter Hendl.

The Jazz Laboratory was created in 1967, supervised by Donald Hunsberger and growing out of the annual summer Arrangers' Workshop and Arrangers' Laboratory Institute.

The Eastman Youth Jazz Orchestra (above), a twenty-three-member ensemble of the Eastman Community Music School, won the Big Band Category in the first annual Charles Mingus High School Competition on 22 February 2009.

Eileen MALONE, *harpist*

Eileen Malone was a
legendary harpist. Her 57
years with the RPO and
ESM is a record.

Jan
DeGaetani, *mezzo-soprano*

Bonita BOYD, *flutist*

with conductor Sarah Caldwell and
composer Samuel Adler

PRISM CONCERTS

Prism concerts, meaning "light reflecting all over the hall," rely
on the unique shape of the Eastman Theatre. They began in
1974 when Rayburn Wright (BM '43) returned from Radio City
Music Hall. Prisms recollect the 1920s shows that George
Eastman set up combining high-class musical shows with

high-class movies,
using the school's
symphony, jazz,
wind, choral, and
chamber music
groups.

One stage group
performs behind
the act curtain
while another is
located in front
of the curtain.
Another group is
in the pit with small chamber-sized groups on platforms on each
side of the stage with the choral people, the jazz people, and
soloists set all over in the orchestra, mezzanine, and balcony.
Groups are lighted individually and dramatically as each performs,
each piece butted up to the next.

Sudden changes in periods, harmonics, or style increase interest.
The coordinator sits in the audience switching from group to
group by raising and lowering spotlights. Three-quarters of the
school may be involved but each group prepares only one piece
about seven minutes long for the hour-long concert.

PARADE *of* MASTERS

Bill DOBBINS, *conductor*
professor of jazz studies and
contemporary media, conducts the
Eastman Studio Orchestra

Zvi ZEITLIN, *violinist*
David DIAMOND, *composer*
John CELENTANO, *composer*

"The Alarm will Sound" GROUP

Ralph STANLEY
and the Clinch Mountain Boys

The Only Game in Town ...

ORCHESTRAS

From 1939 through 1964, the Rochester Philharmonic, usually supplemented by faculty members of the Eastman School, often recorded under the names Eastman-Rochester Orchestra under the direction of Howard Hanson and Eastman-Rochester Pops under Frederick Fennell.

GRADUATIONS

Many colleges and high schools hold graduations in the theater (left). This is the Eastman School's graduation of 2009.

THE LIPIZZANS

In the 1970s and 80s the Lipizzaner Stallions, emulating the Spanish Riding School of Vienna, pranced onto the stage. According to promotional literature, "These are the spectacular leaps and maneuvers, once used by riders in

saddle to protect and defend themselves on the battlefield, which are now preserved as an equestrian work of art. When you see the Lipizzans perform, it is like stepping back four hundred years and viewing one of the greatest equine ballets in history."

The reality was that the horses were kept in a tent where the parking garage is now and a ramp had to be built into the back of the Eastman Theatre to get the equines in to perform their ballet. First, the stage had to be covered with homasote board. Then the homasote had to be painted because shadows were scaring the horses. When the curtain went up, the horses were spooked, RPO veterans recall, and acted naturally just as horses everywhere do.

MAGIC SHOWS

Illusionist David Copperfield and Canadian magician and escape artist Doug Henning were among those who came regularly to the theater. Instead of pulling a rabbit out of a hat, Henning transformed a tiger into a nine-foot tall baby elephant and vice versa. RPO musicians recall that across Gibbs Street where the park is now, there was a restaurant. Henning's trainer was charged with walking the elephant around the block and into the restaurant—a surprise to the other patrons.

Dave BRUBECK, *pianist*

at left in his later years
and below, with his jazz quartet

Eugene LIST, *pianist*

Eugene List hung out with piano-playing presidents and recreated Louis Moreau Gottschalk's Monster Concerts (right). At the gala celebrating the theater and orchestra's 50th anniversary, many pianists played together on the Eastman stage.

List and his wife, Carroll Glenn, taught at Eastman 1964-1975.

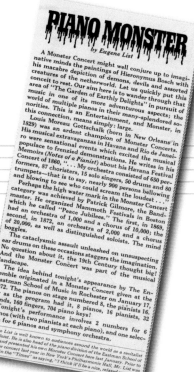

PIANO MONSTER
by Eugene List

A Monster Concert might well conjure up to imaginative minds the paintings of Hieronymus Bosch with his macabre depiction of demons, devils and assorted creatures of the netherworld. Let us quickly put this conceit to rest. Our aim here is to wander through that area of "The Garden of Earthly Delights" in pursuit of music in one of its more adventurous aspects; the world of multiple pianos in their many-splendored sonorities. This is an Entertainment, and Monster, in this connection, means simply: large.

Louis Moreau Gottschalk (born in New Orleans in 1829) was an ardent champion of Monster Concerts. His musical extravaganzas in Havana and Rio de Janeiro were sensational events which excited the musical populace to frenzied demonstrations. He writes in his *Memoirs (Notes of a Pianist)* about his Havana Festival Concert of 1860, "... My orchestra consisted of 650 performers, 87 choristers, 15 solo singers, 50 drums and 80 trumpets—that is to say, nearly 900 persons bellowing and blowing to see who could scream the loudest . . ."

Perhaps the high water mark in the Monster Concert category was achieved by Patrick Gilmore, the Bandmaster. He organized Mammoth Festivals in Boston which he called "Peace Jubilees." The first, in 1869, had an orchestra of 1,000 and a chorus of 10,000; the second, in 1872, an orchestra of 2,000 and a chorus of 20,000, as well as distinguished soloists. The mind boggles.

The cataclysmic assault unleashed on unsuspecting ear drums on these occasions staggers the imagination. No question about it, the 19th Century thought big! And the Monster Concert was part of the musical landscape.

The idea behind tonight's appearance by The Ensemble originated in a Monster Concert given at the Eastman School of Music in Rochester on January 17, 1972. The pianos on stage numbered 8, the pianists 16. Or as the program had it, 8 pianos, 16 pianists, 32 hands, 160 fingers, 704 piano keys!

Tonight's performance involves 2 numbers for 6 pianos (with two pianists at each piano), and one selection for 6 pianos and symphony orchestra.

Eugene List is well known to audiences around the world as a recitalist and soloist. He is also head of the piano division of the Eastman School of Music and presented his own Monster Concert here last January. Prior to a similar concert last year in New York's Philharmonic Hall, Mr. List was quoted in the "Times" as saying, "I think it'll be a nice, relaxed evening."

EASTMAN OPERA THEATRE

Opera at Eastman has come a long way since Vladimir Rosing was reading cue cards in the scenery and a motley crew was assembled in 1925 to put on *Carmen*. Today, the continuous process of producing, instructing, coaching, and directing exposes students to both the traditional opera repertoire and the new lyric theater forms that are now defining the twenty-first century.

Today, under the direction of the Eastman School of Music's voice and opera department, Eastman Opera Theatre presents fully staged productions featuring composers and their music encompassing more than two hundred years of lyric opera tradition. One of these is held in the Eastman Theatre, usually in the spring.

Eastman Opera Theatre performed Le nozze di Figaro *in the Eastman Theatre in March of 2009.*

Renée FLEMING, *soprano*

In 2000, Eastman alumna and internationally acclaimed soprano Renée Fleming (MA '83) performed in the Eastman Theatre, echoing this earlier performance of Don Giovanni, *a production mounted by Eastman Opera Theatre in April 1982 (at left with Jack Warren). John Maloy and Jan DeGaetani were Fleming's teachers at Eastman.*

William WARFIELD, *bass-baritone*

In 2000 Eastman alumnus William Warfield (MA '46) celebrated his 80th birthday with the Philharmonia by reading the words of Martin Luther King from Joseph Schwantner's New Morning for the World.

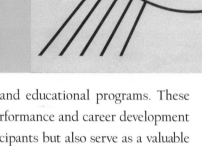

The Golden 20's Gala in honor of George Eastman and the 50th anniversary of the Eastman Theatre and the Rochester Philharmonic Orchestra

PARADE *of* MASTERS

EASTMAN MAKES 'HOTTEST MUSIC SCHOOL' LIST

In the early 1990s, the Eastman School of Music began making the lists of popular magazines rating music schools. At first it tied with other schools but by the end of the decade it was leading the lists as best music school in the country. In the 2008 Kaplan/Newsweek "How to Get into College" guide it was named "hottest music school," citing Eastman students' ability to take additional academic classes in the university's College of Arts, Sciences, and Engineering and to participate in Eastman's Institute for Music Leadership. The guide also noted that applications to Eastman were up ten percent more than the national average. The "Hottest" list recognizes schools with growing reputation and popularity among top students based on admissions statistics as well as interviews.

In a typical U.S. News & World Report rankings of specialty areas among music schools in the United States, Eastman was given the following ratings: first in piano performance, first in music education, first in composition, second in instrumental performance, second in conducting, second in jazz, second in piano/organ/keyboard, and fourth in opera/vocal performance.

Two recent programs illustrate why Eastman is making waves. Since its inaugural competition in 1997, the Eastman Young Artists International Piano Competition has been promoting high artistic standards through the sponsorship of festivals,

In 1973 The Golden 20's Gala celebrated the 50th anniversary of the Eastman Theatre and Rochester Philharmonic Orchestra.

concerts, master classes, and educational programs. These events not only provide performance and career development opportunities for the participants but also serve as a valuable resource to the global community at large.

The other program is the Eastman Center for Music Innovation (CMI) described as "musical leadership energized by taking something traditional and trying it out new." This characteristic is being traced to the school's namesake, George Eastman, an inveterate tinkerer whose "inexhaustible spirit of invention set the stage for entrepreneurship." So far the CMI has created an online music theory course that will be applicable to schools nationwide. It's being advertised as Eastman School's own R&D unit for new ideas in music creation, performance, presentation, science, scholarship, teaching, and commerce.

Eastman School Deans after Hanson...

WALTER HENDL

After Howard Hanson retired, Chicago Symphony Orchestra conductor Walter Hendl, one of the outstanding American conductors of his generation, was named dean. Hendl raised faculty salaries and granted the first paid sabbaticals in the school's history. He brought in noted violinist Zvi Zeitlin and composer Samuel Adler and invited prominent composers Stravinsky, Khatchaturian, and Penderecki for week-long visits. He established the Musica Nova ensemble and encouraged innovative curricula in accompanying, conducting, jazz studies, and electronic music. Controversy and a long personal struggle ended his career at Eastman.

ROBERT FREEMAN

In an era when music schools were trying to define themselves, Robert Freeman brought a new marketing approach to the Eastman aura that called attention to the school's great substance and futuristic ambitions. Freeman initiated a pivotal "Eastman Initiative" that challenged the faculty to think deeply about the future of music, its place in society, and the manner in which a music school should adapt to some of the fundamental changes in musical culture.

JAMES UNDERCOFLER

Following the resignation of Robert Freeman in 1996, James Undercofler, an Eastman graduate, was appointed director and dean of the school and held that position until he resigned in 2006 to accept the presidency of the Philadelphia Orchestra. Undercofler was the principal architect of the Eastman Initiatives, programs designed to give students the skills and experience necessary to meet the demands of performance and education in today's changing musical world. Undercofler's tenure also included an expansion of the *Music for All* program and increased emphasis on technology-based programming.

DOUGLAS LOWRY

On 21 May 2007, composer/conductor Douglas Lowry, formerly the dean of the University of Cincinnati College-Conservatory of Music, was appointed the sixth dean of the Eastman School beginning on 1 August 2007. Lowry had previously served as dean and Thomas James Kelly Professor of Music at the University of Cincinnati's College-Conservatory of Music, and before that as associate dean of the Flora L. Thornton School of Music at the University of Southern California.

The Rochester Philharmonic Orchestra and its parent organization, the Civic Music Association, were distinctive from their inception.

A key attribute that distinguished them from their counterparts was a community-wide membership base exceeding 10,000 in the 1930s. Memberships ranged from five-dollars to major private and corporate gifts largely because of the educational component. The influence of Rochester's successful membership model (as opposed to a wealthy elite-patron model) can be seen in communities all over America today.

Beyond its main classical subscription series in the Eastman Theatre, the Rochester Philharmonic Orchestra and its earlier sibling, the Rochester Civic Orchestra, use the hall for education concerts for school children, as well as for community and pops concerts.

William L. Cahn, author of *Rochester's Orchestra 1968–1995,* believes that the Eastman Theatre was part of the Progressive Era's belief that music is the "grand experience" with the power to raise consciousness. The theater "represents a utopian idea that was present in the 1920s," says Cahn, who experienced it in

The Civic Music Association, parent organization of the Rochester Philharmonic Orchestra, presented singer Marian Anderson several times in the 1930s before she was denied access to the DAR Hall in Washington, D.C., in 1939.

Philadelphia and later in Rochester. "When you make great music available you lift the whole community. From the beginning Rush Rhees endorsed the concept."

The community education component of the core Rochester Civic Orchestra was radical, utopian, and highly influential nationally in the 1930s and 1940s. The prime vehicle for this influence was the orchestra's presence on radio, the central medium of mass communication, for both educational and classical concerts. From the NBC Radio Network broadcasts in the 1930s to the WHAM 50,000-watt broadcast in the 1970s, the subscription series concerts in the Eastman Theatre achieved a national audience.

The close collaboration between the orchestra and the Rochester public schools for music education formed a model for communities throughout America. Further, Cahn says, "it is likely not coincidental that after touring with the Rochester Civic Orchestra, Leonard Bernstein created the monumental CBS Television Young People's Concerts with the New York Philharmonic."

THE FIRST INTERREGNUM

Since the mid-nineteenth century, orchestras have been closely associated with their music directors. Those interludes between the departure of one director and the coming of the next can be a challenging time or an opportunity to savor other conductors.

After Eugene Goossens left in 1931 to head the Cincinnati Symphony, the RPO was five years without a principal conductor. Fritz Reiner served as principal guest conductor, 1931-34, with Sir Hamilton Harty making several appearances. Guy Fraser Harrison, assistant conductor since 1926, and Paul White, principal second violin since 1926, continued to conduct the Rochester Civic Orchestra of forty-five to fifty-five players that was formed in 1929 upon the demise of the Eastman Theatre Orchestra. This orchestra not only survived the Great Depression but actually grew then. Business executive Arthur See moved from the school to head the Civic Music Association.

In 1931 Howard Hanson conducted the premiere performance of William Grant Still's *Symphony No.1 (Afro-American Symphony)*, marking the first time an African-American composer's work had been performed by a major symphony orchestra. Still's ballet *Sahdji* had its world premiere in Rochester the same year. A 1960 recording of the ballet features Howard Hanson conducting the Eastman-Rochester Orchestra. "The close connection between the Rochester Civic Orchestra and the Eastman School through Eastman-Rochester recordings conducted by Howard Hanson and Frederick Fennell, and through the annual American Composers Forum, became the most visible outlet for serious art music created by American composers," Cahn says. "The influence of this collaboration could be found in orchestra programming from the 1920s to the 1970s."

The Civic Music Association, formed in 1929 to succeed the Subscribers Association, sponsored an Artists Series. In his 2009 book *Serving a Great and Noble Art: Howard Hanson and the Eastman School of Music*, Vincent Lenti lists 144 artists ranging from soloists to full orchestras who performed in Eastman Theatre concerts, 1932 to 1972. The Metropolitan Opera made twenty-one appearances, 1934-1960. Among individual artists who made return visits were

Jascha Heifetz, five; Vladimir Horowitz and Fritz Kreisler, seven each; and Arthur Rubenstein, fourteen.

José Iturbi 1936-1944

The charismatic Spanish pianist José Iturbi made a guest appearance with the Rochester Philharmonic in 1934. He was so popular that he was asked to guest conduct the orchestra for two more programs. This led to his being named permanent conductor in February 1936. His popularity continued—indeed

George ENESCU,
composer and conductor

Dimitri
MITROPOULOS, *conductor*

Pierre
MONTEUX,
conductor

PARADE *of* MASTERS

the *Rochester Civic Music News* regularly referred to him proudly as "the world famous conductor." Iturbi was a favorite with the orchestra and they with him. When he came, he had just lost out to Eugene Ormandy for the position of conductor of the Philadelphia Orchestra.

During Iturbi's residence, the orchestra performed coast to coast over the NBC network and in 1937 embarked on its first annual tour. Accolades accrued for educational broadcasts and a recording contract was signed with RCA Victor. Summer concerts were initiated in 1940 and Sunday evening pops concerts continued.

Iturbi started the musicians' pension fund by contributing $500 and donating his services as a solo pianist for a concert that became a yearly affair. He left in 1944 at the height of his Rochester reputation to pursue a lucrative movie career in Hollywood. RPO musicians who sought him out years later found a suntanned and gracious host who invited them into his home to join the party that was in progress. He loved to jabber in Spanish with fellow Spanish musicians such as Juan Figueras, grandfather of WXXI's Julia Figueras.

INTERREGNUM WITH NOTED CONDUCTORS 1944-1947

Upon the receipt of Iturbi's resignation, manager Arthur See immediately planned a brilliant 1944-45 season that included guest conductors Sir Thomas Beecham (three concerts), Fritz Reiner, Igor Stravinsky, Leonard Bernstein (two concerts), Dimitri Mitropoulos, André Kostelanetz, and Guy Fraser Harrison. Beecham took the orchestra on its annual tour that included Carnegie Hall, and the young Leonard Bernstein toured with the orchestra during the next two seasons. Bernstein conducted four programs during 1946-47 and Erich Leinsdorf conducted five. In February 2009, to memorialize her father's association with the RPO, Jamie Bernstein brought four of her father's best-loved musicals to life with the RPO and guest vocalists in the Eastman Theatre.

ERICH LEINSDORF 1947-1956

Throughout his long career Erich Leinsdorf was noted for his exacting standards and acerbic personality. Austrian-born Leinsdorf's first appearance with the Rochester Philharmonic Orchestra was as guest conductor in 1946. In April 1947 he was appointed fourth permanent conductor, remaining for

Leonard BERNSTEIN,
composer and conductor

Louis ARMSTRONG,
jazz trumpeter

the next nine years. His recordings with the RPO garnered nationwide critical acclaim and the orchestra under his baton was described by Carl E. Lindstrom in the *Hartford* [Connecticut] *Times* as "one of the most impressive in the country."

After twenty-two years with the RPO, associate conductor Guy Fraser Harrison left in 1950 to become the conductor of the Oklahoma City Symphony. Leinsdorf left in 1955 but returned as guest conductor during 1956. During the next three years, Pierre Monteux and Leopold Stokowski were among the orchestra's many distinguished guest conductors.

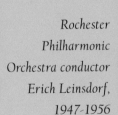

Rochester Philharmonic Orchestra conductor Erich Leinsdorf, 1947-1956

The "Duck Feathers" Caper

The legendary feathers caper occurred at an RPO concert on 14 February 1952. To the chagrin of many concertgoers, Erich Leinsdorf had decided to conclude a lovely program of Mozart, Mahler and Brahms with Tchaikovsky's *1812 Overture*. Moreover, Leinsdorf had instructed that the sound of cannons be simulated by firing a blank pistol into a backstage metal trashcan. After one rehearsal, an orchestra percussionist groused: "It doesn't sound like cannons; it sounds like somebody shooting ducks!"

When the cannons cue was reached at the concert, several loud shots were heard from offstage. Shortly thereafter, a cloud of white feathers emerged from a light port in the ornate theater ceiling above the first rows of audience seats. The feathers descended grandly in the brilliant curtain of light, perfectly synchronized with the descending string passage preceding the final triumphant section of the overture.

A cacophony of confused sounds surged from the audience. The orchestra faltered. Leinsdorf whipped it back into cohesion, finished the piece, and stormed off the stage, thus abruptly ending the concert.

The feathers story spread rapidly. AP picked it up and it went national, including a squib in *Time Magazine.* The plot was conceived and executed by several Eastman School students who were not caught, nor were they identified at the time.

—*written by Charles Valenza*

Arthur RUBINSTEIN,
pianist

Benny
GOODMAN, *clarinetist*

Charles MUNCH,
conductor and violinist

PARADE *of* MASTERS

THEODORE BLOOMFIELD 1959-1963

Theodore Bloomfield (left, being congratulated by Howard Hanson), conductor of the Oregon Symphony, was appointed music director in April 1958 and remained through the next four seasons. He conducted the world premieres of Bernard Rogers's *Variations on a Mussorgsky Song* and recorded Sibelius's *Symphony No. 5* and *Finlandia* with the Rochester Philharmonic Orchestra. During his tenure elementary school concerts were begun, conducted by Paul White. Bloomfield left to take a position with the Hamburg State Opera.

LÁSZLÓ SOMOGYI 1963-1969

Hungarian-born László Somogyi became sixth permanent conductor with the fifteen-concert 1963-64 series, sharing that season with guest conductors Aaron Copland, Walter Hendl, and Leopold Stokowski. Somogyi's post included both music director of the Philharmonic and Civic Orchestra and continued until the close of the 1968-69 season. His comment, "Why use two names for one orchestra?"

led to the examination of a situation that went back to the old Eastman Theatre Orchestra of the 1920s. In 1965 a special report on "Orchestral Music in Rochester" by a study group headed by the Rev. Charles Lavery, president of St. John Fisher College, recommended that "the major emphasis in the future be focused on the Rochester Philharmonic Orchestra and that the Rochester Civic Orchestra as a separate entity be dissolved." Following this advice, the Civic Orchestra's mission of education and community concerts was folded into the RPO's larger mission.

Paul White retired as conductor of the Civic Orchestra in 1965 and Dr. Samuel Jones, whose emphasis was on youth and education, became assistant conductor. Jones wrote and narrated programs featuring actors and multi-media techniques. For three seasons beginning 1969 after Somogyi left, Jones assumed most of his duties with assistance from advisor Walter Hendl, director of the Eastman School of Music.

Also in 1969, a young man from Poughkeepsie came in the middle of a snowstorm to interview and audition for the freshman class at Eastman. Jeff Tyzik took a two-hour tour of the school. "The last stop was standing on the stage looking out into that room with its chandelier," Tyzik recalls, "I was just transformed." Tyzik went on to receive undergraduate and graduate degrees at the Eastman School and has been the principal pops conductor of the RPO since 1994.

Lauritz MELCHIOR, *tenor*

Count BASIE, *jazz pianist and bandleader*

Rudolf SERKIN, *pianist*

Isaac STERN, *violinist*

Chuck Mangione (right) presented "Friends and Love" to a sold-out audience in 1970.

In 1970 composer/arranger and trumpeter Chuck Mangione, an Eastman graduate, presented "Friends and Love" to a sold-out audience. Audience demand for a repeat performance continued to grow over the years and in 2007 the RPO presented three sold-out performances of the Grammy Award winning "Friends and Love." Mangione combined elements of jazz, pop, New Age and even classical music in these performances with the Rochester Philharmonic Orchestra.

Also in 1970, the Rochester Philharmonic Youth Orchestra, a student orchestra under the direction of RPO concertmaster Howard Weiss, was formed. The RPYO continues to perform an annual side-by-side concert in the theater with the professional musicians of the RPO.

William L. Cahn (left), RPO's principal percussionist from 1968-1995, wrote a history of the RPO, Rochester's Orchestra 1922–1989, in 1989.

Joan SUTHERLAND, *soprano*

Dmitri SHOSTAKOVICH, *composer*

Max RUDOLF, *conductor*

PARADE *of* MASTERS

THE CMA REVOLUTION

At the end of the 1960s the orchestra experienced waning support and considerable internal discord. In 1969 a group styled "Save the Orchestra Committee" was organized, but did not have much effect on solving the orchestra's financial or personnel problems.

In January 1972 the Civic Music Association (CMA) informed four players that their contracts would not be renewed after the 1972-73 season, allegedly for musical incompetence. A fifth player, who had been with the orchestra for almost twenty years, was notified that he would be placed on probation. Several of those fired had been prominent members of the local musicians union, including members of its negotiating team and three of them were first-chair players. Significantly, all of these musicians had been outspoken critics of the music director.

The incident brought matters to a head. The players involved demanded reinstatement, alleging unfair labor practices in violation of the National Labor Relations Act. The CMA board backed the director, precipitating a serious crisis for the orchestra, especially since it was in the middle of an annual subscription drive.

In this environment, a group of CMA members, organized by John Santuccio and David Perlman, held a meeting in February 1972 to bring together concerned people in order to determine a course of action. In a series of successive meetings, the group decided to call itself the Concerned Members of the Civic Music Association (CM-CMA), selected its leadership, drafted a platform, and decided to run a slate of candidates for the CMA board in opposition to the official nominees who were to be selected in a proxy vote by the membership at the upcoming annual meeting on 2 October 1972. Their slate consisted of David Glassman, a senior physicist at Kodak; Dr. Grace Harris, an associate UR professor; Eugene List, chair of the Eastman Piano Department; Sidney Mear, Eastman School Professor of Trumpet; Dr. Edward McIrvine, manager of the Physics Research Laboratory at Xerox; Paul Roxin, president of Roxin Radio Communications, Inc.; John Santuccio, a broker with Shearson, Hammill & Co.; Betty Strasenburgh, an Eastman School graduate and faculty member at the Nazareth Academy; Dr. Max Presburg, former Chief of Ophthalmology at Rochester General Hospital; and Charles Valenza, an attorney and holder of a performer's certificate in French horn from the Eastman School. He was also a recent CMA board member, having served from 1964-1970.

Pinchas
ZUKERMAN, *violinist and conductor*
with Mary Zinman and child

Jack BENNY,
comedian and violinist

E. Power BIGGS, *organist*

All of these candidates had great interest in music and most had performance experience. Key elements of their platform were to reinstate the five musicians, "give top priority to hiring good artistic leadership" (David Zinman had been contacted in Holland, and had agreed to become RPO Music Director when an opening became available), revise the CMA bylaws, and "attack the financial problems by hiring a professional marketing manager. . . . [and] beginning a major endowment fund drive. . . ." A formal proxy battle was thus initiated to wrest control of the orchestra from its current leadership at the next annual meeting.

Upon refusal of the CMA board to provide a list of its members eligible to vote, the insurgent group went to court and obtained an order compelling the CMA to make the names available, as required by the not-for-profit corporation law. Margaret McIrvine and Etta Ruth Weigl ran this proxy campaign with great effectiveness and efficiency.

Since the proxy fight was highly controversial, there was considerable ongoing press coverage for many months. The incumbent board leadership refused to concede any points, accusing the dissidents of being lackeys of the union, irresponsibility, and not understanding the dire financial situation that the orchestra faced. The CM-CMA, in turn, accused the incumbent leadership of inept management,

lack of imagination and creativity, and of mistreating the musicians (many of whom had advanced degrees).

As the battle went on, some of the incumbent board members sided with the insurgents, which had the effect of placing complete board control in play. Approximately 500 people attended the annual meeting, which had to be moved to the Eastman Theatre to accommodate them. When the votes were tallied, the insurgent slate won by a margin of almost two to one. Subsequently, many of the incumbent directors who were not up for re-election resigned. The new board then appointed David Zinman music director. The entire Civic Music Association was reorganized, even its name, which was changed to "Rochester Philharmonic Orchestra, Inc."

John Santuccio became president of the RPO and Ted McIrvine was elected chairman of the board and, in large measure, their dedication and leadership saved the orchestra. The lasting accomplishments of the struggle were an era of much improved labor-management relations, a more open management process (including having musician board members), and ultimately, a great improvement in the relationship between the RPO and the Eastman School of Music. The RPO carries on today, nearly forty years later, because of the actions of a few dedicated people.

—*written by David Perlman*

PARADE *of* MASTERS

DAVID ZINMAN 1973-1985

With the 1973-74 season, David Zinman became the RPO's seventh permanent director. By the time Zinman arrived, the Philharmonic had seven outreach programs, including three in the Eastman Theatre: elementary educational concerts; RPO/RPYO joint concerts; and open rehearsals sponsored by the Women's Committee (now the Philharmonic League). Among his achievements during his twelve-year tenure were performances of all the Mahler and Bruckner symphonies, his regular collaborations with soloists Misha Dichter and Itzhak Perlman, and his celebrated concerts with the RPO in Carnegie Hall.

In 1973 Isaiah Jackson was appointed associate conductor, a position he retained until 1985. Jackson became the face of the RPO in the community through his appearances with the orchestra's educational and outreach concerts as well as in the pops series.

RPO director David Zinman (far left) talking with Robert Strasenburgh, chairman of the RPO board

Isaiah Jackson conducts the RPO in 1973 (right)

His performances with actor Robert Forster and taking the orchestra inside Attica and Auburn prisons brought national recognition to the RPO.

Zinman was very strict about honing the orchestra even if it meant overtime rehearsals. He insisted orchestra members avoid playing other programs days before a concert so they could "keep the music in their fingers." But musicians also recall that Zinman wanted to be "one of the boys" during pre-concert lectures. He would casually walk out and sit on the lip of the stage with his feet in the front row of the seats. Maestro Zinman, one of the most popular music directors since Iturbi, announced that he would be leaving Rochester to become the music director at the Baltimore Symphony at the end of the 1984-85 season.

The search immediately commenced for a new permanent director. Orchestra members reacted by nailing Zinman's shoes to the podium. "Maestro was flabbergasted and got very emotional," musicians recall.

The Polish-born conductor Jerzy Semkov, a student of such early twentieth century titans as Erich Kleiber and Bruno Walter, held the position of music advisor and principal conductor, 1985-89. Semkov brought his depth of understanding of the Romantic orchestral classics to his consistently exciting performances.

Duke ELLINGTON,
pianist and composer

Mel
TORMÉ, *singer*

Sir MARK ELDER 1989-1994

British conductor Mark Elder's conducting debut was in May 1986, and in March 1987 Tony Dechario, RPO president, announced that Elder would be the eighth director. Elder concurrently held the position of music director at the English National Opera and this enabled his acclaimed opera concert performances with orchestra and celebrated soloists. Peter Bay was appointed associate conductor. In addition, Bay served as the RPO's artistic director of educational programming for three years. During his tenure in Rochester, Bay conducted more than three hundred performances, among which was the United States premiere of Benjamin Britten's *Concerto Movement for Clarinet and Orchestra.*

George Eastman had imported a bevy of Russians fleeing the revolution during the 1920s for his "International Stew" of the Eastman School faculty; after the Berlin Wall fell in 1989, another Russian contingent began to arrive in the RPO's personnel. Elder's sophisticated musical sensibilities mixed the standard repertoire with new and occasionally challenging works, which he regularly supported with insightful commentary. Knighted in 2008, Sir Mark Philip Elder, Order of the British Empire, has been the music director of The Hallé Orchestra in Manchester, U.K., since 2000.

Martin Luther King Jr Celebrations

Building audience diversity has been an RPO priority since the mid-1980s. In 1985 then-Associate Conductor Isaiah Jackson and Willis Sprattling founded the Martin Luther King Jr. Greater Rochester Commission and began an annual Interfaith Worship Service with the RPO on the King holiday. Community engagement activities have increased in recent years under Charles Owens, current RPO president & CEO. In 2008 the orchestra presented King tribute concerts at Hochstein Performance Hall and Spencerport High School and in 2009 participated in the twenty-fifth anniversary interfaith service at the Eastman Theatre (below). Expanded partnerships with local gospel choirs gave rise to a joyous "Glory of Gospel" concert every spring.

—*written by Charles Owens*

Aram
KHACHATURIAN, *composer*

Alec
WILDER, *composer*

Itzhak
PERLMAN, *violinist*

PARADE *of* MASTERS

ROBERT "BOB" BERNHARDT 1995-1998

Bob Bernhardt, conductor of the Tucson Symphony, was an experimental choice, whose field included classical and opera but also some jazz. Instead of the usual European maestro, the search committee went with an American, born and raised in Brighton, a suburb of Rochester. Bernhardt is currently the music director and conductor of the Chattanooga Symphony and Opera and the principal pops conductor of the Louisville Orchestra.

CHRISTOPHER SEAMAN 1998-2011

Christopher Seaman's thirteen years as music director is a Rochester record. Scheduled to step down after the 2010-2011 season, he will continue an active schedule of guest conducting in North America, Europe and Australia, and also will hold a lifetime appointment as RPO Conductor Laureate. Seaman's availability led to a match made in heaven—he was exactly what the community needed at exactly the right time, said William Cahn who co-chaired the search committee with Eastman School director Jim Undercofler. Why is he so good? First, he attracted more than 500 people for pre-concert chats and that's the envy of other orchestras and cities. His popular "Symphony 101" series at Hochstein Performance Hall was a direct outgrowth of the tremendous early popularity of his pre-concert chats. He's witty; he can sit at the piano and play themes.

The orchestra liked him immediately and he connected with the board of directors. He fit into the community. He thought nothing of conducting the Philharmonic then dashing off to an elementary school and working with kids for an hour or so.

Jeff Tyzik was the young man who wore a sport coat to fend off a blizzard in 1969 and stayed through graduate school and beyond to become RPO principal pops conductor in 1994. Tyzik didn't like the term "pops", thinking it an old term for the dumbing-down of the art form, although acknowledging it is a useful marketing term and an umbrella for film, jazz, Latin music, gospel singing and more. "It's a symphonic experience for those who can't sit through the Verdi Requiem.

Christopher Seaman (left)

Jeff Tyzik (right)

Misha DICHTER, *pianist*

Beverly SILLS, *soprano*
Michael TILSON THOMAS, *conductor*

Jan PEERCE, *tenor*

Jessye NORMAN, *soprano*

They can sit in a beautiful room and hear a wonderful orchestra play music of high artistic integrity. They don't have to worry about protocol or if they are wearing proper dress or when to clap."

The orchestra continues its long tradition at the vanguard of music education. Michael Butterman was named principal conductor for Education and Outreach (The Louise and Henry Epstein Family Chair) in 2000, the first position of its kind in the country. In addition to performing concerts for students of all ages, RPO musicians visit virtually every elementary school in the Rochester City School District through the Primary Ensembles Program.

Under Maestro Seaman's leadership, the RPO has received numerous accolades and awards, including the New York State Governor's Arts Award for excellence and community service. In 2005 and 2006, the American Society of

Composers, Authors and Publishers (ASCAP) and the American Symphony Orchestra League honored the RPO with an ASCAP Award for Adventurous Programming, recognizing the orchestra's commitment to music written in the last twenty-five years.

An aerialist with "Cirque de la Symphonie" and the RPO, 2009

Left to right: Suzanne Welch, Arild Remmereit, Charles Owens

ARILD REMMEREIT TAKES THE PODIUM

The appointment of Norwegian Arild Remmereit as the eleventh music director of the Rochester Philharmonic Orchestra, beginning September 2011, reinforces the artistic excellence of the orchestra and the importance of its place in the greater Rochester community.

Remmereit's appointment also harkens back to the orchestra's initial concert in March 1923 that starred Alf Klingenberg, Norwegian-born pianist of great distinction, playing Grieg's *Piano Concerto*. As first director of the Eastman School of Music, Klingenberg attracted many compatriots such as Christian Sinding to the founding faculty of the new school.

RPO president and CEO Charles Owens remarked that the 2010 search committee was "dazzled by [Arild Remmereit's] energy, passion, and visionary ideas on the role a symphony orchestra can play in contemporary society."

The announcement of a new music director was made by RPO president and CEO Charles Owens on 15 September 2010 in Kilbourn Hall (right). RPO board of directors chairperson Suzanne Welch stated, "The standards were set high, and I am proud to say Arild Remmereit fits perfectly."

The Orchestra plays with such a high artistic integrity, beautifully nourished by Christopher Seaman for these past 13 seasons. I look forward to building upon the historic foundation set by my predecessors.

—Arild Remmereit

CONCLUSION

In its eighty-eighth year, the RPO presents more than 150 concerts per year, serving approximately 500,000 people through ticketed events, education and community engagement activities, concerts in schools and community centers throughout the region, and broadcasts on WXXI 91.5 FM. The orchestra performs with the Rochester City Ballet, Mercury Opera Rochester, and Empire State Lyric Theatre. It collaborates regularly with the Rochester Oratorio Society and Eastman-Rochester Chorus, and mentors the Rochester Philharmonic Youth Orchestra (RPYO).

Inspired by the combination of George Eastman's love of music and his sincere interest in the cultural enrichment of his community, the RPO throughout its history has been an industry leader in the close relationship between the organization and its community.

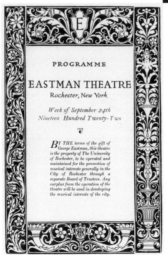

The Subscribers Association of the 1920s expanded into the Civic Music Association in the 1930s and became the Rochester Philharmonic Orchestra in 1975, using the initials RPO. The RPO remains a membership association with the ultimate management control in its members, which now number in the thousands.

This is what made it possible in the 1970s to have a major change in management through membership voting, a change which over a generation ago introduced a number of innovative management ideas, such as having orchestra players on the board of directors, and much more collaboration between the orchestra and management in dealing with orchestra matters. As an example, in 2009 orchestra members began participating in selecting a new music director.

The RPO, having been based throughout its history in the Eastman Theatre, has carried out George Eastman's desire that the theater and its orchestra be used, as an early "Programme" (left) suggests, "in developing the musical interests of the city."

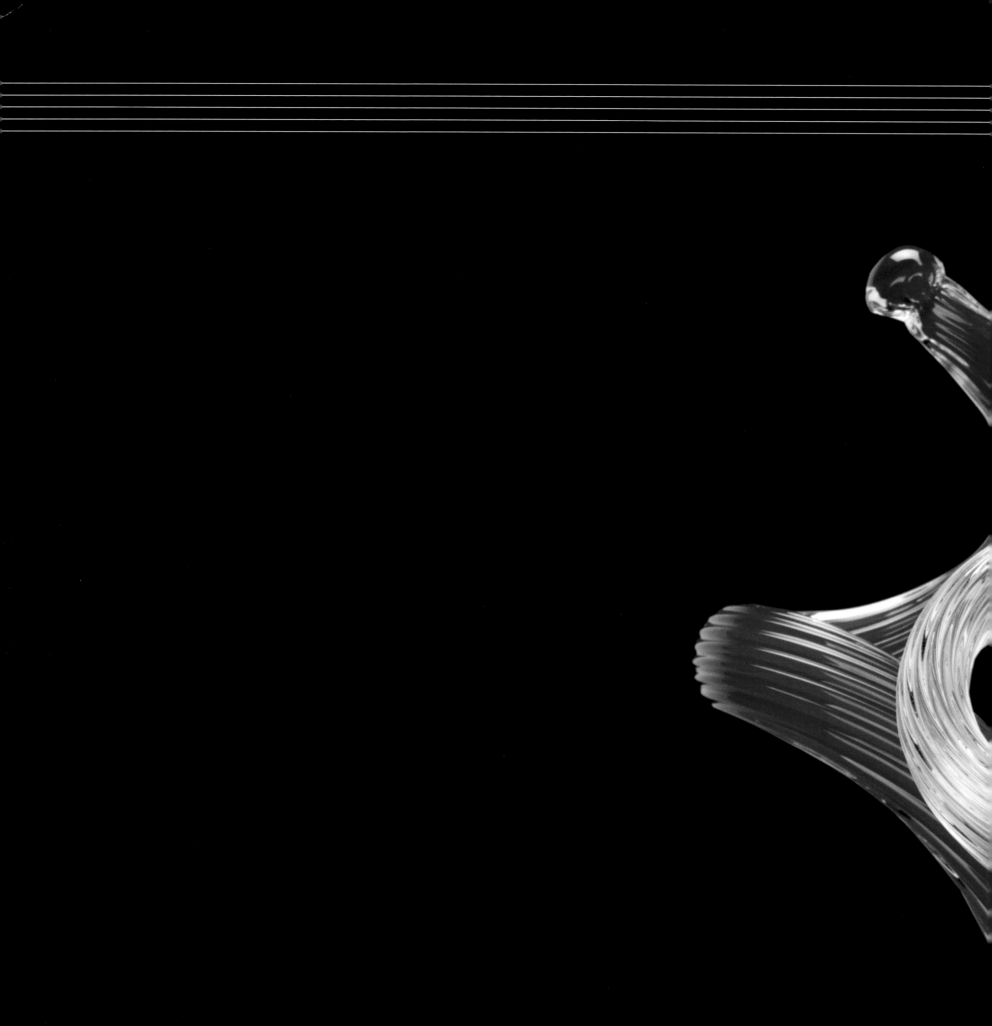

PART THREE

The Majesty Grows

RENOVATION AND EXPANSION

This year, Strasenburgh and her allies will drum up support for the Eastman School and Eastman Theatre projects. —Stuart Low, 2001

George Eastman's first photograph in 1877 was of Rochester. The scene was the Genesee River looking south from the aqueduct that carried the Erie Canal and focused on the bend in the river where the University of Rochester would rise in the 1920s—thanks to Eastman's largesse. The ambrotype passed to Henry Alvah Strong who labeled it "GE's first Photo." And it is the Strong name—as in Strong Memorial Hospital or Strong Health—that has driven the University of Rochester to become the community's largest employer in the twenty-first century, succeeding "The Kodak City" of the twentieth century.

FOR THE ENRICHMENT OF COMMUNITY LIFE is inscribed on the corner façade of the Eastman Theatre. Rush Rhees probably crafted the axiom, although Eastman himself constructed some snappy aphorisms, witness the Kodak slogan "You press the button, we do the rest." But Rhees's axiom certainly represented the donor's wish for community involvement.

The late well-known architect Robert Macon designed many buildings for the Eastman Theatre neighborhood. Above is a detail of his rendering for the renovated Kodak Hall at Eastman Theatre.

The community was involved from the beginning in the 1920s with the new orchestra that played in the Eastman Theatre. The involvement came through the Subscribers Association that became the Civic Music Association and then the Rochester Philharmonic Orchestra, Inc.

Community input and momentum returned during the past fifteen years with the evolution of the current plans for the Eastman Theatre expansion. In a sense, the late well-known architect Robert Macon started it all: Macon designed many buildings for the Eastman Theatre neighborhood. Some were built—houses in the Grove Place neighborhood, Symphony Terrace, and Eastman Place. Some were not built, such as his proposed mid-size theaters in the parking lot diagonally across from the Eastman Theatre. Some were merely postponed until after his death, such as his plans and elevations for the renovation and expansion of the Eastman Theatre. In order to understand how the final theater plans developed, it is necessary to first consider their relationship to the proposed performing arts center.

A PUSH FOR A PERFORMING ARTS CENTER

By the mid to late 1980s, local performing groups were urging the development of a multi-venue Performing Arts Center (PAC). The potential community benefits from such venues were apparent. The Eastman Theatre, built as a

Eastman was the creator of snappy aphorisms such as "You press the button, we do the rest" for the first Kodak camera in 1888. His first photograph (below) of a decade earlier was taken from the Main Street Bridge; in the far distance we see the spot where the medical school and undergraduate campus of the University of Rochester would move with his financial help, 1920-1950s.

movie palace, had deficiencies as a concert hall, being too large and having acoustical problems. There was no other suitable concert hall in the community. In addition, Rochester had never had a suitable mid-size venue for opera, music, theater or dance.

By the mid 1990s, an unofficial local group had been formed to develop a specific proposal for a Performing Arts Center. Its leaders included James Undercofler, director of the Eastman School of Music; Robert Macon, architect; Betty Strasenburgh, ESM graduate in harp, member of the RPO and Eastman School boards; Max Jenkins, a member of the East End Alliance; Fred Gregory, a vice-president of the RPO; Charles Valenza, Eastman School of Music alumnus, former county attorney and former RPO board member; and David McDonald, local industrialist and RPO board member. The group met more or less twice a month for two years at Strasenburgh's neighborhood home on Grove Street beginning in March of 1997.

Anticipating the Eastman Theatre's potential role as a major venue in a future Performing Arts Center, in 1997 James Undercofler engaged consultants to ascertain the improvements needed to make the theater suitable for touring shows. The study recommended updating and expanding the theater to include the parking lot at the corner of Main and Swan Streets, and ironically was not unlike—in template and basic content—the current Eastman Theatre expansion.

During the same period, the Rochester Broadway Theatre League (RBTL), having separated from the Rochester Philharmonic Orchestra, was lobbying for a new, large theater to replace the Auditorium Theatre for the presentation of Broadway shows and other pops attractions. It developed a specific proposal for a Performing Arts Center to be located in the High Falls district, west of the Genesee River.

In early 1997, the New York State legislature appropriated $425 million for Community Enhancement Facilities Assistance, which included arts and cultural facilities. The legislation provided that one third each of this sum would be allocated to projects designated by the governor, the president pro-tem of the Senate, and the speaker of the Assembly. Local legislators soon recognized that state funding would not be allocated unless the community agreed on a single project proposal. Jack Doyle, county executive, and William Johnson, Rochester mayor, jointly appointed a thirty-one-member committee of cultural, business, educational, community, and governmental leaders to investigate the need and feasibility of new and/or improved performing arts facilities, and to make recommendations concerning such facilities and their location. The committee engaged a nationally recognized consulting firm, a theater architect, and an acoustician to assist in its work.

Both the performing arts group and RBTL made formal presentations of their recommendations to the joint city-county committee. The performing arts group recommended a four-venue PAC consisting of the Eastman Theatre for road shows, and a 1,958-seat concert hall and 1,142-seat theater for opera and dance designed by Robert Macon to be located in the parking lot diagonally across from the Eastman Theatre; and a 300-seat "Black Box" theater to be located in the expanded Eastman Theatre. RBTL recommended a three-venue PAC consisting of a 2,500-seat Broadway roadhouse, a 1,000-seat community theater, and a 500-seat experimental theater, all located in High Falls.

In March 1999, after approximately one and a half years of work and often strenuous debate, the Committee of 31 presented its report, recommending a plan for a PAC with a large theater of 2,500+ seats, a concert hall of 1,200-1,800 seats, and a 900-seat hall for small groups and experimental productions. The committee recommended that the Eastman Theatre be retained as an integral part of the PAC, and that venues be clustered close to each other in the vicinity of the Eastman Theatre. Theater and acoustical consultants had reported to the committee that

while the Eastman Theatre could not be turned into a "world class" concert hall without essentially reconstructing its interior, it could function well as a Broadway roadhouse, and at lower cost than new construction.

After the Committee of 31 submitted its report, the future of the PAC was relegated to a 5-person committee consisting of two county employees, two city employees and one member of the former Committee of 31. This new committee over the next two years with very little, if any, public participation ultimately formulated a plan featuring a 2,800-seat Broadway roadhouse in Midtown Plaza, a 900-seat playhouse for theater and dance, and a 200-seat studio theater. The plan did not address the Eastman Theatre. Efforts made by various performing groups to include a mid-sized theater located in the parking lot diagonally across from the Eastman Theatre failed, ostensibly because of the cost, but also because of disagreements among various potential users as to its governance, design, and utilization.

Enter and Exit Renaissance Square

In 2001 the Rochester Genesee Regional Transportation Authority (RGRTA) proposed a transit center on Main Street between Clinton Avenue and St. Paul Street, combined with a high-rise office building, commercial retail space, housing units, and a parking garage. The transit center proposal ran into heavy opposition and appeared to be going nowhere when suddenly in 2003 a new plan called Renaissance Square surfaced to combine the transit center with a new Monroe Community College (MCC) downtown campus, and what was described as a Performing Arts Center. But the site was only large enough to accommodate the bus station, the MCC campus and a 2,800-seat Broadway roadhouse. By the fall of 2009, the Renaissance Square project had collapsed.

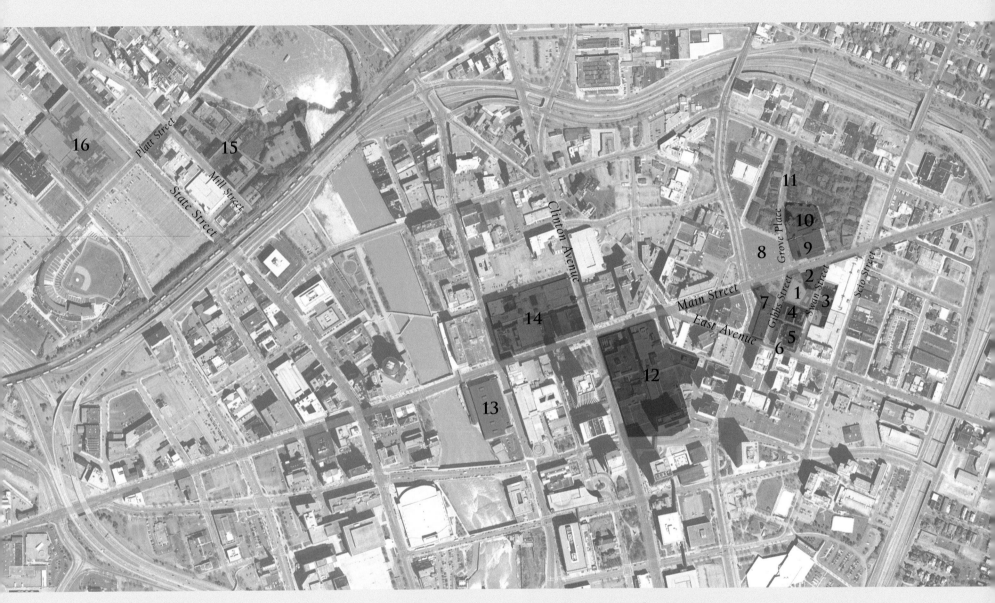

1— Eastman Theatre

2— Eastman Expansion Site

3— Eastman Annexes 1 & 2

4— Eastman School of Music (ESM)

5— Eastman Community Music School

6— RPO Office

7— Miller Center (Eastman Place)

8— Parking

9— The Y (YMCA)

10— ESM Student Living Center

11— Grove Place Neighborhood

12— Midtown

13— Convention Center

14— Proposed Renaissance Square Site

15— High Falls District

16— Kodak Offices

ᎡHE EASTMAN THEATRE GOES IT ALONE

In the meantime, the unofficial group meeting at Betty Strasenburgh's home forged ahead in its support of major renovations at the Eastman Theatre. In March 1999, the same month that the Committee of 31 (of which James Undercofler was a member) made its final report, the Eastman School of Music board of managers was discussing renovations, which would include improvements to the theater's lobby and acoustics, and an enlarged stagehouse, dressing rooms and rehearsal hall. This would allow for Broadway productions, although the theater's primary use would be for the Eastman School of Music and Rochester Philharmonic Orchestra.

By October 1999 the estimated cost of the theater renovations had greatly increased. Betty Strasenburgh and a number of her friends offered substantial, but conditional, lead gifts. But in a memo to the Eastman board, James Undercofler stated that the Eastman Theatre renovations should be considered an integral part of the Performing Arts Center project planning. Undercofler cautioned, "To move ahead independently now on the redevelopment of the Eastman Theatre would be ill advised. We must know the design of the other theaters in the Performing Arts Center before adopting any single plan."

This memo prompted a response from Betty Strasenburgh listing seven concerns and objectives that needed to be agreed upon before she and others would make a final commitment to their gifts. One objective was that the project proceed according to the plans prepared by Robert Macon. One concern was that tying the renovations of the Eastman Theatre to progress on the public Performing Arts Center deliberations was likely to cripple the theater renovations by endlessly delaying the project, given the uncertainty surrounding the progress of PAC planning.

In October 2000 the Eastman School of Music contemplated a $40 million fund raising campaign, $20 million of which was to be used to renovate the theater. In January 2001 Stuart Low wrote an article in the *Democrat and Chronicle* headlined "Performing Arts Center Waits in the Wings." In a subsequent article, Low wrote, "This year Strasenburgh and her allies will drum up support for the Eastman School and Eastman Theatre projects." During the rest of 2001, however, doubts were raised concerning the progress, if any, toward building the community PAC. In August 2001 Charles Valenza, in a report to county executive Jack Doyle, indicated his serious concern that the PAC project appeared to be focused solely on the con-

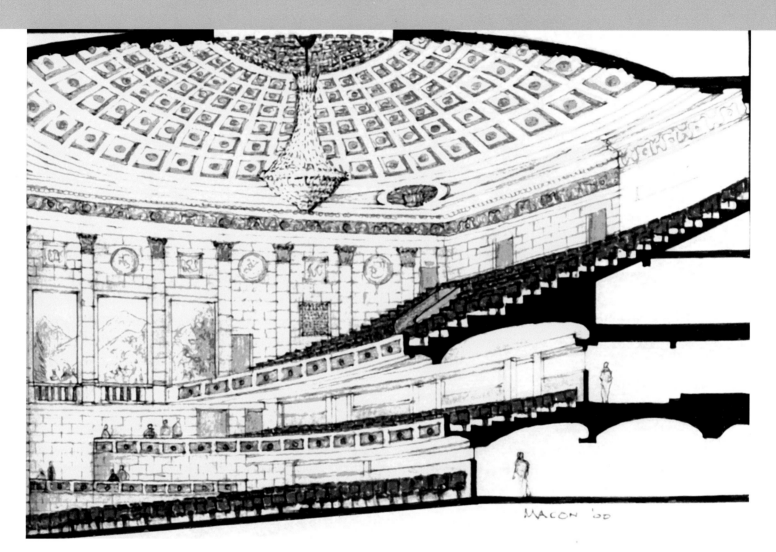

struction of a large Broadway roadhouse and that other smaller venues recommended by the original joint city-county committee would never be built. Op-ed pieces to the same effect also appeared in the *Democrat and Chronicle*.

During 2002 it became apparent that the Eastman School fund raising campaign was not going well. However, Betty Strasenburgh contributed $100,000 to move forward with theater construction drawings. Subsequently, university president Thomas Jackson suggested a phased program in which only the "stage" component would be authorized, and that any further

work on the theater would be considered as a two- or three-phase project. Shortly afterward, Betty Strasenburgh met President Jackson at the checkout counter in Wegmans and pleaded with him to move forward with the entire project at one time.

After a formal meeting with President Jackson in November, Betty Strasenburgh sent a letter to the University of Rochester Gift Office on December 9 expressing her doubts as to whether the theater project as originally represented to the board of managers was either financially feasible or had the necessary support of the university to become a reality. In January 2003

I've conducted in multi-purpose halls around the world and they are, without exception, disastrous. If you build it right for symphony, you can adapt it for everything else. If you build it for everything, it's not right for anything.

—Christopher Seaman

James Undercofler wrote the Eastman board that authorization for construction drawings for the addition and recital hall would be put on hold, and that the project would be broken up into phases, which presumably would be completed over a five year period. Four days later, Strasenburgh resigned as co-chair of the Campaign Committee for the Eastman Theatre Project. The project, she decided, was, for all intents and purposes, dead.

In March 2003, the Eastman School Development Office conducted a series of interviews and came to the conclusion that while interest remained high, the levels of potential giving were less than reported in a study done two years earlier. The forward movement of the project fund raising seemed to halt. The Eastman School of Music did not even have a development director. Betty Strasenburgh was not involved either; instead, she bought a boat and went cruising.

Still, the first phase of the project, a $5 million renovation of the stage to enhance the visual and acoustical experience of both performers and audience, was completed in 2004, but apparently not then fully funded. This included a new custom shell, upgraded stage lighting, a new computerized rigging system, and an improved orchestra pit with all-new mechanics and hydraulics. Implementation of the second and third phases would prove more challenging and would wait until a new university president, Joel Seligman, arrived. (See chapter 10.)

After a three-year hiatus, in June 2006 Strasenburgh met with Seligman and started lobbying all over again for the renovations and additions to the Eastman Theatre. Joining her at this meeting were Dr. Jamal Rossi, then acting dean of the Eastman School of Music, and Roger Friedlander, a trustee of the university and member of the Facilities Committee as well as a board member of the Rochester Philharmonic Orchestra. Betty Strasenburgh stressed how important the expansion was and how critical it was to start immediately. The counter argument was that the university should wait to see what would happen with building plans of other local groups and the Performing Arts Center supported by the county and city governments. Another year went by without much progress on the theater. Ultimately the Strasenburgh view would prevail—that the needs of the Eastman School of Music and the Rochester Philharmonic Orchestra should be considered without regard to other arts groups involved in the public Performing Arts Center planning.

As 2007 dawned, President Seligman and Dr. Jamal Rossi presented to the board of the Rochester Philharmonic Orchestra a plan for Phase II of the project estimated to cost $20 million. They asked for RPO help in raising funds. This proposal included adding boxes along the theater's sides to improve acoustics, reducing seating from a little over 3,000 to 2,250 seats, adding restrooms, and a café on the main floor. It recommended a small new building on the east side of Swan Street for addi-

Macon's
drawings for the
new atrium show
a soaring five-
story space
topped by glass
and steel and
crisscrossed by a
bridge or bridges
that connect the
mezzanine level
of the Eastman
Theatre with the
recital hall and
the balcony level
of the theater
with the
rehearsal hall in
the new wing.

MACON '00

tional instructional and rehearsal space for the school. But it did not include the proposed additions designed by Robert Macon—atrium, recital hall, and an orchestra rehearsal hall—to be built on the parking lot at the corner Main and Swan Streets. The Macon additions were relegated to a future Phase III.

At a March 2007 meeting of the RPO Executive Committee, Betty Strasenburgh spoke passionately about doing Phases II and III together, pointing out that the university's $20 million Phase II plan would not meet the needs of either the Eastman School or the RPO. Former RPO board member Charles Valenza, after reviewing the $20 million proposal, explained that it would be highly unlikely that the Phase III additions would ever be done after Phase II, leaving the Eastman School and the community with an inferior facility.

Discussions were held between President Seligman and other university representatives and representatives of the RPO. The main topic was getting the RPO's help in raising money. Soon the RPO Executive Committee suggested a paragraph be added to the university's proposed Memorandum of Agreement with the RPO stating that if funds were available, the option for completing Phase III should remain viable. An RPO delegation of Elizabeth (Betsy) Rice, Suzanne Welch, Keith Wilson, Janet Newcomb (then interim RPO CEO) and attorney Frank Crego of the Harter Secrest firm met with President Seligman, Ronald Paprocki, Rob Gibson, Dr. Jamal Rossi, and legal counsel Sue Stewart to discuss the memorandum. The agreed outcome of this meeting was to add a paragraph stating, "If fund raising is successful, the option for Phase III remains viable."

About a month later, Betty Strasenburgh with her friend Eugene Van Voorhis met with State Assemblymen David Gantt and Joseph Morelle to enlist their support for an additional $5 million from the state. The assemblymen had previously obtained, with the support of the entire local legislative delegation, an $8 million grant for the theater project. Morelle and Gantt said they would support the additional grant, but only on condition that the whole project, including the Phase III additions, were to go forward at the same time. When Betty Strasenburgh met with President Seligman three days later to discuss the additional $5 million the assemblymen would work for, he enthusiastically supported completing all the proposed renovations and additions to the theater as one project. Soon the university's trustees approved the entire project, too.

On 10 September 2007, the university held a press conference in the parking lot at Main and Swan Streets to announce that the university, with the RPO's support, would be undertaking the entire project of renovations and additions to the Eastman Theatre, including Phase III, and to thank the local state legislative delegation for obtaining the additional financing from the state. The next day, the *Democrat and Chronicle* stated that renovations were to take place during the summers of 2008 and 2009 and the Phase III additions were expected to be ready for use in the fall of 2010. Prior to announcing the public fund raising campaign, the university had obtained a pledge of $10 million from Eastman Kodak's Economic Development Fund. (See chapter 9.)

The press conference on 10 September 2007 announced that the university with the support of the RPO would be undertaking the entire project of renovations and additions to the Eastman Theatre, including Phase III, thanks to many of the people pictured here (left to right): Catherine Carlson, Dr. Jamal Rossi, Joseph Morelle, Craig Jensen, Joel Seligman, Betty Strasenburgh, Nancy Macon, Douglas Lowry, Roger Friedlander, Susan John.

PART THREE: THE MAJESTY GROWS

155

On 8 October 2009, the opening night RPO audience progressed into the renovated Kodak Hall at Eastman Theatre behind John Beck on a 1922 snare drum. The festivities recalled not just the theater's opening on 4 September 1922 (see page 39) but also George Eastman's photographs of this very spot ça. 1878 (see page 159).

How can a city this size afford this beautiful hall and such musical quality?

—Antonio Perez

THE NEW KODAK HALL

On the balmy evening of 8 October 2009, RPO percussionist John Beck rum-a-tum-tummed a snare drum to lead opening night guests into the renovated Kodak Hall at Eastman Theatre. The drum was original to the theater in 1922. Watching that procession, some people had thoughts that went back to the same area 130 years previously. What is now the confluence of Main, Gibbs, Grove, and Selden Streets was then a grove of trees through which a country lane wound to an Italianate villa occupied by George B. Selden, whose invention of an internal combustion engine presaged the automobile age.

When George Eastman approached that future confluence ça. 1878 to take lessons in wet-plate photography from Selden, he did not know that he would purchase the area forty years hence for a music school and movie theater. Instead, as part of his lessons, he took photographs of the grove of trees, the winding lane, and the Selden house. Those photographs

Music has always been important to Kodak CEO Antonio Perez (above): He sang in choirs as a youth; he played classical guitar; and he listened to good music in the world's finest concert halls. Perez considers the Eastman Theatre the jewel in the crown of this community and "an important tool to use as a global company in attracting the best possible talent."

were later given by Selden's son to the Department of Rare Books and Special Collections of the University of Rochester.

ANTONIO PEREZ MUSES ABOUT KODAK HALL AT EASTMAN THEATRE

As a European lucky enough to travel and work in seven different places around the world, Kodak chairman and CEO Antonio Perez knew well the great concert halls— La Scala, Carnegie Hall, those in Berlin and Barcelona. He also knew the one in "my little hometown of Vigo [in Spain], a community about the size of Rochester" and expected the Eastman Theatre to look "more like [the Vigo] hall." He knew about the Eastman School of Music "but not how important it was." When he considered all the musical activities in Rochester and then walked into the Eastman Theatre for the first time, "it was truly a phenomenal surprise." His initial thought was, "This doesn't belong here," and his next thought was, "How can a city this size afford this beautiful hall and such musical quality?"

The downside came when Perez received his first Rochester Philharmonic Orchestra tickets and sat in the mezzanine seat that was George Eastman's: "The sound was terrible. I was hearing but not enjoying the music." His first impulse was to change seats "but then it dawned on me that I could not publicly reject the symbolic honor of sitting in the founder's seat" just because of an acoustical problem.

THE BEAUTY OF THE GROVE OF 1878: In 1940 George Selden's son recalled when "a slight young bank clerk who painted as a hobby" came to his father's house and mounted the stairs to the attic studio for photography lessons. "In an outburst of enthusiasm, the artist [Eastman, at left] suggested the beauty of the grove which surrounded the house as a subject for the camera. A series of photographs were made [below], no mean undertaking with the slow wet plates."

Improving Acoustics...

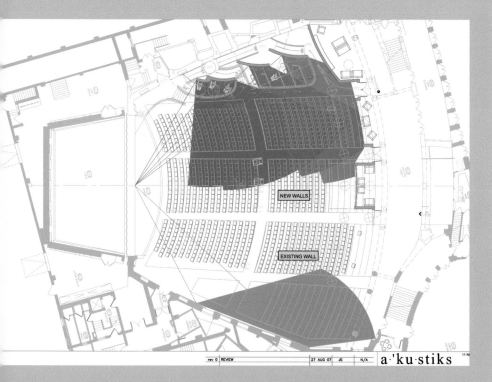

NEW WALLS

EXISTING WALL

rev 0 | REVIEW | 27 AUG 07 | JS | N/A | a·'ku·stiks | 11 M

This concept drawing shows how the acoustics in the Eastman Theatre would be improved by the renovation. Gold indicates the state before the renovation when lateral energy did not reach the seats but was absorbed by the Zenitherm walls. The red, violet, blue and green arcs show how the new curved boxes redirect energies from the stage into the audience.

Then the new University of Rochester president, Joel Seligman, appeared "out of nowhere" at Perez's office and the two discussed being "inevitably united by George Eastman and committed to taking his legacy to the highest level" they could. Seligman's plan was that they could complete the founder's vision while fixing the sound and size of Kodak Hall—the name that would unite the company Eastman created with the renovated concert hall in the Eastman Theatre. Fortunately, Seligman asked for the money before the worldwide economy collapsed.

Music has always been important to Perez personally: He sang in choirs as a youth; he played classical guitar; and he listened to good music in the world's finest concert halls. After reading up on Rochester and George Eastman before becoming Kodak CEO and meeting with Seligman, Perez decided that the Eastman Theatre was the jewel in the crown of this community and "an important tool to use as a global company in attracting the best possible talent." By supporting the theater, "it shows employees that we are completely committed to this community."

"I couldn't imagine any name but 'Kodak Hall,'" Perez says now of the outcome of that first meeting with Seligman.

Music continues to enthrall Perez. He recollects how concertmaster Juliana Athayde, "a jewel of a performer," played Vivaldi's *Four Seasons* at the announcement of the $10-million for Kodak Hall from the company's Rochester Economic Development Fund, which was created in 2004 to invest in community projects. Athayde faces the Kodak Box on the second tier of boxes and always waves when Perez, his wife and young daughter appear in the box. In that box, too, is George Eastman's reupholstered mezzanine chair with its built-in hat rack and a guest chair—two of the four he always reserved.

Mitch Miller complained that "Eastman lacks reverberation."

Perez recalls warmly the last RPO performance before the hall closed for renovations. "Maestro Seaman asked what I would like to see performed." Perez immediately identified Carl Orff's "magnificent" *Carmina burana* (in which he had sung as a youth), "If you have the guts," he added. Perez then bought lots of tickets for invited friends and family from both sides of the Atlantic, and they all listened happily to Orff's famous scenic cantata.

A later example of the intimacy the theater exudes since its renovation came at the grand opening of 8 October 2009. (See pages 178-179 and the Kodak Moment, 174-175.) Perez's young daughter was able to identify her doctor among the Rochester Oratorio Society members assembled to sing that iconic work of power and freedom—*Beethoven's Ninth*. Many other Rochesterians also experienced the more intimate and cozy atmosphere that resulted from eliminating more than 750 seats.

Perez's prescription for the future of the Eastman Theatre is simple: "As members of this community, we should be thankful to George Eastman for creating this jewel and see as many performances as we can to keep it full and healthy."

Acoustics Through the Years

"The RPO people are constantly complaining about the acoustics," remarks Donald Hunsberger, professor emeritus of conducting and ensembles. "It's as hot a topic as political elections."

It was ever thus. Rochester architect Will Kaelber's frustrated remark to New York architect Larry White that "we will never recover if we fail to produce a hall that is acoustically perfect" set the stage. Paderewski and others "pronounced the acoustics perfect like those of Kilbourn Hall," Eastman reported to his acoustician, F. R. Watson of the Department of Physics at the University of Illinois. On 5 September 1922, the morning after the theater opened to the public, Eastman telegraphed Watson: I WISH TO EXPRESS MY GREAT APPRECIATION OF YOUR SERVICES… DEFECTIVE ACOUSTICS WOULD HAVE RENDERED THE EXPENDITURE OF THE VAST SUM INVOLVED PRACTICALLY USELESS. The subject went underground for a generation until reopened by the likes of Mitch Miller, who complained that "Eastman lacks reverberation" and David Zinman who faulted the Zenitherm walls as "acoustical cardboard that soaks up sound like a

While loud passages of music are always very impressive, the real magic occurs at the edges of silence. For instance, in Debussy's "Afternoon of a Faun" where there is a whole six beats of nothing, you don't want to be hearing mechanical systems.

—Christopher Blair, acoustician

sponge." Zinman made some practical suggestions such as removing the carpeting, corrugating the back of the [Izenour] stage shell so the brass did not sound so constricted, and tipping the shell itself to reflect the strings.

"A question of Eastman Theater's acoustics" announced a 1980 newspaper headline. The discussion was raging then despite a 1971-72 multi-million dollar renovation of the theater that included the new shell designed by George C. Izenour (see page 95) that was meant to solve the problem of stage acoustics but instead made it worse.

The article compared the size of the theater with its 3,094 seats to other concert halls—in Boston, New York, Chicago, Syracuse, and Buffalo—all of which were smaller and built for symphonic concerts. Renovating the Eastman Theatre as a true concert hall might have involved the destruction of the beautiful murals and endangered the gilded ceiling and magnificent crystal chandelier, some news articles said.

"Cirque de la Symphonie" and the RPO, 2009

Piano virtuoso André Watts performed Beethoven's Concerto in E-flat major for Piano and Orchestra, Opus 73, familiarly known as the "Emperor Concerto," with the RPO at the opening concert on 10 October 2008. As a child, Watts's piano-playing mother encouraged him to emulate the virtuoso pianist Franz Liszt and to adopt Liszt's love of practicing and theatrical playing style.

Yo-Yo Ma rehearses in the Eastman Theatre with the Rochester Philharmonic Orchestra. Ma played the Dvorak Concerto in B minor for Cello and Orchestra, Opus 104 on Monday, 5 May 2008.

A Truly 'New Hall' Emerges

"This is a new hall," said Christopher Blair, principal of the Akustiks firm in Norwalk, Connecticut, in describing the acoustical renovation of venerable Eastman Theatre during the summers of 2008 and 2009 in preparation for the RPO's grand opening on 8 October 2009. "New in sound, for both the orchestras that play on its stage and the audience that sits in its reconfigured auditorium," Blair continued. He had been on the job since 2002 and worked on the stage renovation of 2004 designed by architect Robert Macon.

More than 750 seats were permanently removed during the renovation of Kodak Hall for a more intimate experience. Hand rails were installed for safety in the mezzanine, loges, and balcony.

From this angle, one can see the rarely noticed medallions of famous composers on the face of the loges, pictured left to right: Mendelssohn, Mozart, Chopin, Liszt, Verdi, Brahms, Tchaikovsky, Wagner. Medallions not pictured include Schubert (see page 96), Schumann, MacDowell, Haydn, Gluck, Haendel [sic], Palestrina.

The architectural firm Chaintreuil Jensen Stark Architects, LLP designed the Eastman Theatre renovations. Back row, left to right: Partners Craig Jensen, AIA, Dirk Schneider, AIA, and Robert E. Stark, AIA; front row, left to right: Project Managers Rory Welch Zimmer and Michael J. Ellison, CSI

The Pike Company, which built the original theater, 1919-1922, was also responsible for the renovation of the theater and the construction of the new wing, 2004-2010. Left to right: Tom Judson, owner and CEO; Len Bower, executive VP; Mike Flannery, operations director; Norm Rockefeller, project manager; Tom Sawyer, project superintendent

After the stage was done,

it made the sound less distant to the public.

Everyone has noticed that and

it makes the whole concert experience better.

The next phase will give an enhanced clarity

so the sound pops. —Christopher Seaman

 Phased Renovation

The Eastman Theatre renovation was done in phases, says architect Craig Jensen, who became the partner-in-charge after Macon's death in 2002. The work was phased because the architects were working for the Eastman School and the Rochester Philharmonic Orchestra, both of whose seasons correspond to the school year. "We had a four-month window during the summer months of 2008," Jensen said, "then had to wait for the summer of 2009 to continue."

Jensen is described by Kodak's CEO Antonio Perez as "a brilliant young man who wants to keep the spirit, integrity and especially the idiosyncrasy" of the original theater intact while improving its acoustics, seating, and intimacy.

The first phase, completed in 2004, replaced the acoustically failed shell of the 1970s designed by George C. Izenour, prominent professor of theater design and technology and director of the electro-mechanical laboratory of Yale University. But there was very uneven response on that stage: certain players couldn't hear anything because there was nothing over their heads and the sound was all deflected out into the room. The ultra-heavy shell was awkward for stage crews to manipulate and the huge towers took up platform space.

The new 2004 shell solved these problems and reflected the architecture of the room. It is easy to remove and completely automated. The rear wall flies up, the side walls fly up and

2010
Recalls 1922
Construction...

The renovation and construction of the Eastman Theatre during the summers of 2008 to 2010 recalls the original construction of 1922 in sight and sound. Back then a gigantic swung scaffold was built from a small forest of timber and suspended from roof tresses. The interior of the nascent theater before and after its Labor Day opening exuded total sensory bombardment worthy of a Marrakech bazaar. Early on, all of the trades set up fully equipped noisy shops in the auditorium. The clang of hammer and chisel rose from marble cutters as they cut, trimmed and polished the stone. Metal workers and steam fitters were busy as was a large workshop of artisans casting and shaping sculptural and ornamental plaster. The installation of the largest Austin theater organ in the world and the testing of its pipes were under way.

The buzz of saws indicated that the timber was being cut into 2,755 two-by-twelve inch planks fourteen feet long. The swung scaffolding thus built made a platform seventy feet above the floor, 135 feet wide at the Gibbs Street end, 74 feet wide at the stage end, and 115 feet deep. It had to be strong enough for the men and materials all the trades loaded on to it.

The fifty tons of ornamental plaster coffers, graded to become larger in a series of circles from the central sunburst to the base were cast on the projection booth or second balcony level for forty workmen to mount from the scaffolding onto the huge shallow dome whose diameter spanned 135 feet.

out—all in about four minutes. The design of this shell is more closely aligned with the closure at Boston Symphony Hall in terms of the shaping and height of the ceiling, but it has some additional diffusive elements to bring the energy down. Acoustical ports (windows) can be adjusted to vent some energy from louder instruments, such as the tuba.

"The present stage with its new shell is much livelier," says Donald Hunsberger. "It's almost loud when you're on stage. It used to be that the best sound was in the balcony because the sound sort of transferred itself over the orchestra seats. Now, it seems, depending on the group that's on stage, it's reversed. It's gotten better just from that Roman Forum shell."

During the summer of 2008, air conditioning and infrastructure work was done, and during the summer of 2009, the reconfiguration of the hall was completed to further improve the acoustics. The pit lift system was overhauled with adjusted levels to make it more functional.

The theater's interiors walls of Zenitherm—a thermal material that insulates exterior walls but also absorbs sound—were coated with polyurethane in 2004 to benefit acoustics. (Since RPO music director Christopher Seaman had always wanted more high frequency response from the stage, he had said that if some scaffolding was provided, he would personally paint that Zenitherm.) The new stage set continues the Zenitherm theme visually but is painted plywood.

Acoustician Christopher Blair worked on the new Laura Turner Concert Hall (2006) in the Schermerhorn Symphony Center (1870) in Nashville, Tennessee. Craig Jensen and ESM and RPO people traveled there before tackling the renovation of the Eastman Theatre.

There are special challenges in dealing with a space this large, Blair and Jensen say. The volume of the Eastman Theatre is similar to that of the Metropolitan Opera and Carnegie Hall and when you get a large volume like that, you generally try to preserve as much energy as you can; having absorbent walls was just throwing away the high frequency energy.

The new stage solved many of the problems but there were others, present from the beginning, due to the fan shape of the hall. As is apparent in Blair's diagram (page 160), lateral energy (represented in yellow) did not get thrown back into the center. "This is a fairly good condition for drama, speeches, lectures, or movies, where you don't necessarily want to be surrounded by sound," Blair explains. "But this is a music school and so we

Over the summer of 2009, construction crews worked to transform Kodak Hall at Eastman Theatre into a twenty-first century acoustical marvel while honoring its history and maintaining its historic character. Concrete and steel box seats on the left and right sides of the orchestra and mezzanine levels are being installed. The old seats are gone but the new ones have not yet arrived.

The chandelier was said to have 585 lights, a number Eastman School historian Vincent Lenti remembers because it is also the (current) Rochester area code.

proposed to reshape the lower portion of the room. The balcony and loge areas had always been considered to be pretty good, so the idea was 'Let's not mess that up.' We came up with a series of curved masonry boxes to redirect the sound. Farther out in the room you get the overlapping energy. We've also reconfigured the rear wall and reduced the seating. This frees up space in the lobby, which is a major corridor for Eastman students and faculty. There was always the potential for interference between the walking activity and the rehearsal activity on the stage. What we did is visually open the corridor to the theater with windows but still acoustically seal it off. Another solution would have been to create a wall from balcony to floor, but that would have created a flat-back of energy to the stage; instead we shaped this wall with a lot of ins and outs. The energy that comes back from, say, a snare drum sound hitting the wall doesn't come back as a harsh slap but more as a push. Musicians need to feel they have a connection to the room; this late return is important to them, which was the reason this wall was developed as a very bumpy surface with seating areas. But we still have glass partitions and we still have the flexibility to close off those areas with curtains for some pops acts where you want to make the response of the room a little less strong."

"With this solution we are also capturing all the sound in the space," Jensen adds. "Previously when the lobby was open to the auditorium, the sound just disappeared. Now there is a lot more presence of the sound on the floor and the audience will be enveloped in it."

The 2,326 new seats (down from the former 3,094) have been selected specifically for their acoustical qualities. They are also more comfortable: spacing has been expanded and the reverberation time has gone up. It was about 1.5 seconds, but for symphony music you typically like something closer to 2.0. By reducing the number of seats, potentially the reverberation time goes up. "We wanted that," Blair says. "The seat backs are three inches higher to provide a little more absorption for the empty-seat condition with rehearsals. Otherwise, the room would be harder to use for rehearsals when there's no one sitting in the seats. We've moved to a solid wood seat bottom and back. All of these changes come into play. The wood bottoms preserve more of the double bass energies." Carpeting deadens sound: In the orchestra and mezzanine, energy has been lifted with very thin carpeting remaining only in the aisles. Blair continues:

"So in addition to the sound sounding better, with the new mechanical systems the hall is quieter than before, indeed impressively quiet within the constraints of existing conditions. While loud passages of music are always very impressive, the real magic occurs at the edges of silence. For instance, in Debussy's *Afternoon of a Faun* where there is a whole six beats of nothing, you don't want to be hearing mechanical systems, " he said.

"There's a limited amount of space in the basement below the theater so fans and the like can't be put in Schenectady. The bigger they are and the farther away they are, the quieter they are. But the existing level of noise has dropped by half."

Temperature and especially humidity affect acoustics. If the room gets really dry, such as it does in winter, it begins to absorb high frequencies more. That was another reason for sealing the Zenitherm walls. The new air-handling system tries to even out the humidity over the year because that affects the instruments, particularly the soundboards of pianos and string instruments. Stable humidity is even more important than stable temperature. The goal is forty percent humidity.

Air conditioning was introduced ça. 1926-27 and revised a year or so later with noisy nozzles because people were (figuratively) dying of the heat. Steam heat radiators on the walls that go bang-bang have been disconnected and heat is delivered differently now.

Some of the new ambience comes from new lighting, such as that spotlighting the murals. The flaking paint of the murals has been stabilized by a conservator.

In addition to everyone "listening to the hall," there was a last fine tuning session before opening night. In these final sessions, Blair conducted the orchestra and sent the music director out into the room and up into the balcony to see how the final product sounded. "We worked together in adjusting the hall and the orchestra," said Blair.

The ribbon-cutting on 7 October 2009 brought many of the major players of the Kodak Hall story together. President Seligman admonished all to "rededicate ourselves to continuing the nation's finest school of music in one of the world's most outstanding venues 'for the enrichment of the community.' " Front row, left to right: Charles Owens, Douglas Lowry, Joel Seligman, Mrs. Robert (Peggy) Wegman, Susan John; middle row: Joseph Morelle, Betty Strasenburgh; Antonio Perez, (person obscured), Thomas Hildebrandt, Christopher Seaman; back row: Craig Jensen, Thomas Judson, Ronald Paprocki, George Hamlin, Richard Pifer, Dr. Jamal Rossi, David Gantt

THE KODAK MOMENT

8 October 2009: The audience is filing in and soon Maestro Seaman will lift his baton for the world-premiere of Geo by Dean Douglas Lowry. "Such an auspicious occasion deserves the best of the old and the best of the new," Seaman wrote, "and tonight we have both....There is plenty of festive celebration in this [Geo] music; heard in the powerful fanfare-like figures near the beginning; there is also energy, enthusiasm, and humor, particularly in the delightful Vienna waltz-like section. Mr. Eastman would have been proud to see his School and his Orchestra collaborating like this—teamwork which has brought about the renovation of his Theatre."

George Eastman and friends relaxing at Oak Lodge (below, left); pictured from left to right are Mary Mulligan, Ada Hubbell, Maria Kilbourn Eastman, Walter Hubbell, George Eastman, Edward Mulligan.

A section of the score from Geo (below)

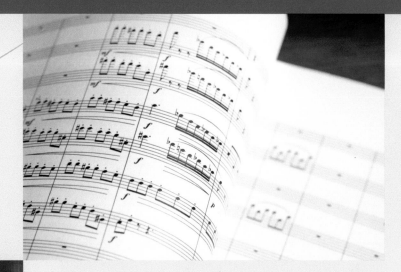

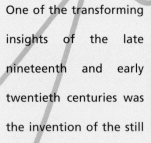

One of the transforming insights of the late nineteenth and early twentieth centuries was the invention of the still photograph, the closest approximation of a viewed image heretofore known. George Eastman transformed the still photograph not only into a global business enterprise, but also a burgeoning art form.

Still symbols, though, sometimes seek motion. Narrative prose becomes a stage play; the still photograph becomes a 'motion picture.' *Geo* is an homage to a man who, as we know, 'built' the Eastman Kodak Company, created the Eastman School of Music and its original Eastman Theatre, and was a cornerstone founder of the University of Rochester and the Rochester Philharmonic Orchestra. Eastman was also a seminal force in the transformation of the still photograph into moving pictures. *Geo* pays tribute to George's dream, revitalized as Kodak Hall at Eastman Theatre, yet also salutes Eastman's cinematic spirit in a style of music that moving pictures ultimately inspired. The Eastman Theatre was conceived not only as a concert hall, but as a movie house.

Geo begins as George's ghost is awakened with a clarion call from the brass. Startled at the clamor, he sits up only to see his Theatre transformed into a modern performing space, its grandeur intact, its dimensions perhaps a little more intimate than the original house. George's ghost darts around the room, through the crystals of the chandelier, beaming up and around the murals and icons, and finally comes to rest, at which point he gazes down on the reclining ghost of his

Douglas Lowry receiving accolades after the world premiere of Geo on opening night of the newly renovated theater, 8 October 2009 (left), and at the piano on the Eastman stage (below).

mother, Maria Kilbourn [Eastman]. (The orchestra plays a slow simple elegy to Maria.) George summons Maria to a waltz; as is the nature of some dances, the waltz gets complicated, and George and Maria swirl around the hall in a kind of impressionistic frenzy. Worn out, they sit down, take note of George's 'new' hall, and listen as the orchestra romps through the celebratory bustle of the twentieth century. After the opening musical panorama reprises in a loud and brassy finale, we imagine the ghost of George Eastman standing and tipping his hat to us in the audience. We hope he is happy.

—*Geo* as explained by its composer, Douglas Lowry, for *Bravo*

Geo *was commissioned by the Rochester Philharmonic Orchestra and its distinguished music director Christopher Seaman.*

Finally the hush lived expectant and the concert of great style and beauty began. The Rochester Oratorio Society under the direction of Eric Townell performed with the RPO in Beethoven's Ninth. Christopher Seaman wrote: "For the Finale, a mere orchestra was not enough for Beethoven, so he adds four soloists and a chorus in a setting of Schiller's Ode to Joy."

How pleased George Eastman would be to know, 86 years later, that these two institutions he loved so deeply would be thriving, respected throughout the world and united in this unprecedented effort.

—Charles Owens, President and CEO, RPO

Years of Uncertainty

The four-year time lapse between the stage renovation in 2004 and the resumption of construction during the summer of 2008 reflects years of uncertainty as to whether the renovation program would include a freestanding building on Swan Street with a large rehearsal hall and six faculty studios. In that case such amenities as the box office and first floor restrooms would need to be incorporated into the already crowded theater building. Then massive sound-deadening materials around pipes would be needed. (Water is an excellent conductor of sound.) If an addition to the theater itself was possible, amenities could be planned in new construction and the box

Joel Seligman (left) said that the "visionary Betty Strasenburgh [right]…was particularly significant in galvanizing political and community support."

office and lobby to the new recital hall could be on Main Street.

If this new separate building on Swan Street for rehearsals were built, Room 120, a large rehearsal hall in the Eastman School near Kilbourn Hall, could be converted into a small recital hall. This would have been a compromised solution, not accomplishing all that was hoped for, including size. One of the concerns the faculty had was the height of Room 120 ceiling being only 22 feet. Additional constraints were isolation from activities and no access to the outside. It would have meant losing rehearsal space without getting an optimal recital space for students—which was one of the primary needs and goals. By moving the project to Main Street, existing rehearsal space in the Eastman School was also preserved.

The result is an architecturally significant new wing of 32,000 square feet.

Joel Seligman Inspires Progress

"Let me take you back to 2005 when I first visited the Eastman School and was given a tour of the facilities," said University of Rochester president Joel Seligman. "I was impressed on the one hand by the beauty of the core Eastman Theatre and on the other hand with how tired it seemed. The real fatigue was in the less visible parts, the teaching parts, the parts you didn't see, the rabbit warren upstairs.

The construction crews that perform high in the sky are not unlike the "Cirque de la Symphonie" performers in the Eastman Theatre. (See pages 141 and 162.)

The beginning of construction of the new wing in 2008 looks not unlike the beginning of construction of the Eastman Theatre in 1919 (see page 28) except the trucks and building materials are up-to-date and there are no scurrying rats from displaced grocery stores.

"Then what impressed me as I talked with those who performed in the theater was that they would talk about the inadequacies of the acoustics. I was startled by that because there was great pride in the $5 million [stage] shell but there was still a long way to go. So I started spending some time listening to music while sitting in different places. There were dead spots—spots where the music was harder to hear.

"I became a convert to the notion of renovating and expanding the Eastman Theatre for two reasons. The one was to give a booster shot to a great school of music about which I am totally passionate. The other was this is [the university's] leading illustration of our commitment to the Rochester community. The first reason was probably more important to me and probably more important to the board. Our fiduciary duty starts with a commitment to our students and their academic mission. We really did hope that this would inspire progress in downtown. But it starts with [the fact that] the Eastman School really is a jewel of the University of Rochester and we were going to do everything we could to protect that jewel."

In 2005 Phase I (the stage) of the renovation and expansion plans was complete but not yet fully funded. There were no plans in place to finance the rest, estimated then to cost an additional $35 million. Five years later, the whole project was

estimated to cost $47 million. "We pursued financing the project through a combination of state government grants, private donations including the Kodak $10 million, and university debt," Seligman continued. "The $13 million [obtained through state legislators] is the lynchpin. The university's board of trustees was the residual financier and they were willing to loan up to $17 million."

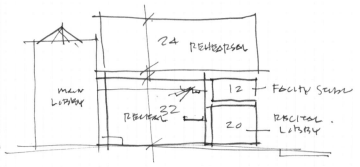

"It's like building a house, brick by brick," Seligman said. "Some people see certain aspects; others see different pieces or portions. At some point, they all have to come together if the project is to succeed. It requires an awful lot of things to work simultaneously."

Steel beams are hoisted up by crane; iron workers grab the attached strings and guide the beams into their designated locations (above).

The wing reaches its height of five stories (above, right).

Architect Craig Jensen's quick section drawing of the halls in the new wing shows the importance of ceiling heights to the acoustics of the spaces (right).

Metal decking is placed on structural joists; this decking will serve as the substructure for a portion of the new roof (right).

After confirming that the building steel is plumb, iron workers weld beams into their final resting spot (below).

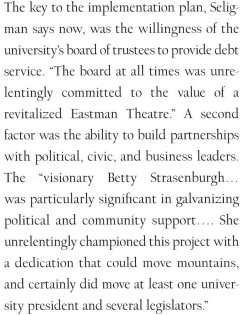

The key to the implementation plan, Seligman says now, was the willingness of the university's board of trustees to provide debt service. "The board at all times was unrelentingly committed to the value of a revitalized Eastman Theatre." A second factor was the ability to build partnerships with political, civic, and business leaders. The "visionary Betty Strasenburgh… was particularly significant in galvanizing political and community support…. She unrelentingly championed this project with a dedication that could move mountains, and certainly did move at least one university president and several legislators."

Soon there was a total of about $30 million in pledges for the entire project, including commitments from the Davenport-Hatch Foundation, the Wegman Family Charitable Foundation, the Louis S. and Molly B. Wolk Foundation, Catherine Carlson, Roger B. and Carolyn T. Friedlander, George and Mary Hamlin, Ron and Sharon Salluzzo, and many others.

After the money was raised, the challenge became how the construction could be made to proceed. Much of the credit there goes to Dr. Jamal Rossi, senior executive associate dean of Eastman School of Music, who acted as overseer of the project, and Elizabeth (Betsy) Rice, RPO board liaison to the project management team.

Topping Out Ceremony

The traditional ironworkers' *Topping Out Ceremony*—signing the final beam (left) before it is hoisted into place atop the Eastman Theatre addition (right)—occurred on 28 May 2009. Representatives of the RPO, Eastman School, the university and the community spoke during a deluge. Then all attendees signed the beam in permanent ink. Speaking for the community, Betty Strasenburgh noted the debt owed to the late Robert Macon, whose designs were being faithfully carried out by architect Craig Jensen.

The late architect Robert Macon's son, Peter, and widow, Nancy (right)

The topping out ceremony is common in England, Germany, Czech Republic, and Poland, and was brought to this country by European craftsmen. The height of the ceremony takes place when the last piece of steel, painted white and signed by all, is lifted into place and secured. The evergreen tree on top, an ancient Scandinavian custom, symbolizes growth and brings luck.

Hatch Recital Hall is going to be magnificent because instead of having to put twenty-first-century acoustics into a twentieth-century building as with the Eastman Theatre, you will have twenty-first-century acoustics in a twenty-first-century hall.

—*Joel Seligman*

Hatch Recital Hall

By moving the recital hall to Main Street, the frontage of Eastman's three major performing halls—Kilbourn Hall, Kodak Hall, and Hatch Recital Hall—open to the two major public streets, Gibbs and Main, that George Eastman chose for their public view.

Even so, it's not enough to just be new because "there are plenty of newly built structures that are not acoustically great," according to Dr. Rossi. Conversely, "there are great halls from a good many years ago. But," Rossi concludes, "we have a keener understanding of how design affects acoustics than we did one hundred years ago."

Hatch Recital Hall is intended primarily for students although it will be open to use by community groups, too. "This doesn't preclude others from using Hatch Hall," Dean Douglas Lowry said, "but the primary reason for doing this is to take some of the pressure off Kilbourn. It also creates a special venue for a particular kind of music, i.e., an intimate repertoire of chamber

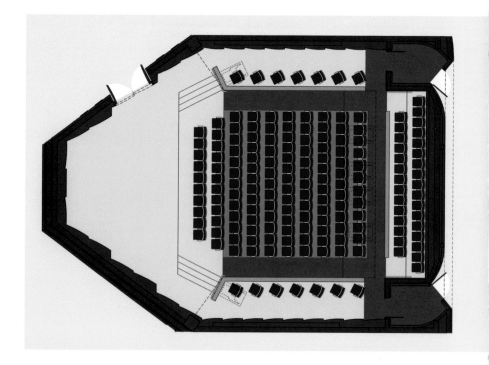

music and solos. When you try to do more and more things, you have to make more and more compromises. So this was designed definitively for solo and chamber music. No matter what technological advances take place in the next fifty to one hundred years, students are still going to stand on stage with a piano and a violin and there are still going to be string quartets and other traditional ways of making music," Lowry concluded.

Hatch Recital Hall with 222 seats complements and supplements Kilbourn Hall with its 455 seats. Kilbourn is world-renowned as a wonderful acoustical space. Howard Hanson Hall with its 65 seats is also a recital space. The Eastman School opened in 1922 with about 400 students. There are now almost 900 students, all of whom are required to give recitals. This adds up to more than 700 recitals, including ensembles, each year. "We can't accommodate them all in Kilbourn Hall," Rossi said.

Hatch Recital Hall (opposite page and left) has walls consisting of cherry dowels behind which a sophisticated adjustable acoustical system lurks. The stage can handle up to twelve performers at once. A mezzanine level adds extra seating.

The roof line above the main entrance to the theater lobby (below) poses a conundrum because these are the only tiles on the roof line.

In addition to audience size, the primary difference between Hatch Hall and Kilbourn Hall is that Hatch is acoustically isolated in its own structure: nothing else touches it. Typically a structure has columns and beams. In an ordinary room, a beam serves as the ceiling of one room and the floor of the one above it. "You have to imagine a sealed box," Rossi said. "Hatch is its own building with its own foundation, its own walls, its own ceiling. All the other structures on the upper floors of the new wing surround it but don't touch it. Whatever happens above doesn't transfer down. One-and-one-half-inch-thick dry wall insulation further sound-proofs the hall. If an ambulance goes down Gibbs Street, you'll hear it in Kilbourn Hall but not in Hatch Hall."

"Hatch Hall also has adjustable acoustics," Rossi said. "It's a fabulous system and one of the reasons for the cost of the project." Depending on the ensemble, the acoustics can be adjusted.

For forty years, the Eastman School had talked about building a recital hall. There's a study that former dean Walter Hendl commissioned in 1970s about building a recital hall in that

Hatch Recital Hall is a discrete building.

Over there, two inches away from this building,

is another building and between them is a rubber gasket.

That's the only thing that connects these two buildings.

—Dr. Jamal Rossi

parking lot. Until now, students either gave their recitals in Kilbourn Hall or in the Ciminelli Lounge of the Student Living Center, which is a beautiful space but not a world-class recital hall. Now, all students will be performing in world-class spaces.

Hatch Recital Hall is designed for about twelve persons maximum—such as the "Appalachian Spring" ensemble—on stage. "We don't want to see a big band in there although a jazz combo might be great. The volume of the space is designed for, say, classical guitar which won't have to push to create sound. Singers, brass quintets, some jazz ensembles will fit—but not a full orchestra which would overpower the room and be too much sound for the space. Sound is energy and the volume of the room can accommodate just so much energy," explained Rossi.

The aesthetics of Hatch Recital Hall never change. The door from the lobby to the recital hall features cherry dowels over solid wood. The cherry dowels of the walls look like louvers but behind them is a ten-foot wide cavity in front of an acoustical hard surface that is made of double-layered dry wall. If you want a space that's really live, a space where the sound goes in and bounces back out—for instance at a solo guitar recital—you can arrange things behind the dowels so that it reflects sound.

There is an acoustical banner that sits below floor level behind the cherry dowels and can be raised all the way to the ceiling if necessary. That absorbs sound so that when the sound goes in, it doesn't reflect back out. It can be completely hard or completely covered by the banner (perhaps for a brass quintet) being raised up by a motor in the ceiling. A string quartet might have the banner completely down. It's all on computer. If you want the setting for piano, you just put it in the computer. There is a preset for guitar. If the sound is too bright,

you move or tune the banner to get the sound you want. You've probably been in recital halls where the curtains are drawn or they're not, but here no one is ever going to see any curtains. The aesthetics of the hall never change because it's all behind the grid of dowels.

Directly above the Hatch Recital Hall, which seats 222 including upper-level seats and is 32 feet high, is a rehearsal hall, serviced by two elevators large enough to move grand pianos.

Rehearsal Hall

The large rehearsal hall on the fourth floor seats a full-size orchestra and is 24 feet high. This hall is the same shape and slightly larger than the Eastman Theatre stage and has a maple floor, thirteen doors—a lot with vestibules and storage rooms with curtains for instruments. There is one opening to the small lobby.

Sound-proofed behind miles of insulation and one-and-one-quarter-inch drywall that rises the full 24 feet, the rehearsal hall is not penetrated by the sounds from the recital hall below or a fire truck on Main Street.

Three Batiste Madalena posters decorate a wall of Betty's Café (left).

Faculty Studios

Six new studios for the Eastman School faculty are on the third floor. Because of the trapezoidal shape of the lot and building and the curve of interior and exterior walls, each studio has a different shape.

The Eastman School faculty were concerned that they be able to use all the new spaces simultaneously in whatever way they chose without transferring any noise or vibration. Craig Jensen, architect, and Christopher Blair, acoustician, developed a solution to structurally isolate each from the other. Thus, each of these new studios has its own little space and is a box inside of a box and doesn't touch any of the rest of the structure. In turn, Hatch Recital Hall has a concrete ceiling and the rehearsal hall above it has a concrete floor. The air between the concrete slabs muffles all sound.

The new wing provides double-acting support services for multiple users in terms of elevators, rest rooms, and handicapped access for the theater. Previously, there was no handicapped access to mezzanine or balcony levels in the Eastman Theatre and no restroom on the main or orchestra level. New restrooms have been installed on all levels.

Betty's Café

Long a wished-for amenity, a small café of twelve tables with four chairs at each table has opened along the Gibbs Street wall of the enlarged theater lobby. It and the new lounge areas were made possible by the removal of seats at the rear of Kodak Hall and by the conversion of a long-neglected exit lobby, formerly known as "The Hall of Mirrors."

The solid doors along Gibbs Street have been replaced by glass to give the café a lighter, more open feeling. Wi-Fi is provided so that Eastman School students may use the tables at times when the café is not serving food.

Fittingly, the café is decorated with three Batiste Madalena movie posters. (See pages 66-67.) More than eighty years after Madalena's posters were unceremoniously dumped into a mud puddle on Swan Street by Paramount-Publix, reproductions have been purchased by the university and ceremoniously returned to their rightful home. All Madalena ever wanted was to be the best movie poster artist in Rochester. How surprised he would be to learn that with all the posthumous honors, exhibitions, and soaring prices his works now command, he is in contention for consideration as the best movie poster artist in the entire world.

"Betty's Café" is so named in honor of Betty Strasenburgh and dedicated to her father, Albert C. Bloomberg.

The Wolk Atrium with Chihuly Sculpture

The expanded theater includes the new five-story Wolk Atrium featuring a magnificent large-scale glass suspended sculpture created especially for the space by the renowned glass sculptor Dale Chihuly.

"Dale Chihuly is certainly one the most innovative, influential and celebrated artists in contemporary art," said Grant Holcomb, the Mary W. and Donald R. Clark director of the Memorial Art Gallery of the University of Rochester. "His work is found throughout the world and in most, if not all, major American art museums. He is a true phenomenon who, for over half a century, has transformed the concept of blown glass in contemporary sculpture."

The curved first-floor promenade north of the Hatch Recital Hall and Wolk Atrium offers patrons covered access from Swan Street into the new building and on to Kodak Hall at Eastman Theatre. The glass wall provides a view of Main Street from inside and a view of the Chihuly sculpture from outside.

A new Main Street entrance opens into this new link and enhances pedestrian flow, including wheelchair accessibility, between the new wing and the oval lobby of the historic Eastman Theatre. Four Psyche and Cupid wall panels (see pages 112-115) have been installed in this new link. The new Eastman Theatre box office here has four stations or windows. A small gift shop features books, CDs, DVDs, and tourist items. From the floor of the Wolk Atrium, stairs and elevators lead to the upper part of the new addition and the Eastman Theatre.

Under construction, the five-story atrium ending in a skylight from which the Chihuly sculpture will hang (right)

Stairs lead up to a bridge that overlooks the new Wolk Atrium. The late architect Robert Macon was greatly influenced by I. M. Pei and his East Wing of the National Gallery in Washington, D. C., which features an Alexander Calder mobile. Macon always hoped the Eastman Theatre would have a Chihuly in the atrium; this sculpture was given anonymously in Macon's memory. During the planning process, university president Joel Seligman noted similarities between the magnificent Chihuly in its soaring limestone and glass space (the best of the new) and the splendid vintage chandelier that hangs from its golden sunburst in Kodak Hall (the best of the old). Both are icons of their periods. Visible in daylight from Main Street, the Chihuly is theatrically lit from without during hours when the theater is in use rather than from within as the typical chandelier is.

Then up to a small recording control room. In all there are five levels: the first three are very public; the fifth level is really minor. Mechanicals are huge because it is important to have a really quiet building.

Dale Chihuly's biography credits him with moving away from creating the small, precious object and moving into the realm of large-scale sculpture. Chihuly embraces collaborative endeavors in which he puts together teams of artists with exceptional glassblowing skills. He develops complex multi-part sculptures of dramatic beauty that investigate translucency and transparency.

In early 2010, the sculpture was assembled at the Chihuly Studio in Seattle, Washington for approval (below–far left). In October 2010, the final installation in Eastman Theatre's Wolk Atrium was completed by a team from his studio (as seen in the remaining series of photos on this page).

The Wolk Atrium with the Chihuly sculpture as seen from inside (left) and outside (above) on preview night, 13 October 2010

The artist Dale Chihuly himself explains the magic of his "chandeliers" when he writes: "What makes [the sculpture] work for me is the massing of color. If you take hundreds or thousands of blown pieces of one color, put them together, and then shoot light through them, now that's going to be something to look at! When you hang it in space, it becomes mysterious, defying gravity, becoming something you have never seen before."

Detail of the exterior of the Eastman Theatre (left)

Architect's rendering of the exterior of the Eastman Theatre with the 2010 addition (below)

George Eastman's original vision was to place a world-class music school in a structure alive with professional music and other arts. —Douglas Lowry

THE LAST WORD

Dean Douglas Lowry reflected on the significance of the history and renovation to the future of the Eastman Theatre: "The Eastman School of Music is unique in the pantheon of leading music schools in America in that a prominent professional orchestra is rehearsing and performing in our building. Eastman students can sit in on great orchestra conductors and soloists; many Eastman faculty members are in the orchestra.

"The new wing creates opportunities for attracting new students and enhancing the educational experience for students and thousands of patrons. The aesthetic/sonic beauty of the grand, elegant Kodak Hall in addition to Hatch Hall and the new rehearsal space is visually and acoustically stirring. Students taking lessons in one of the new modern studios will walk back to the school through the special sky-lit atrium with its Chihuly sculpture.

"Eastman envisioned the consummate multi-media institution. He was always tinkering. Part of his vision was a school and professional, performing orchestra that would work in synchrony—a wonderful mix of students and professors as part of the fabric of the city."

So we come full circle back to music as a spiritual necessity for George Eastman and his desire that the Eastman Theatre be used "for the enrichment of community life."

With Appreciation

We are grateful to the following individuals for contributing their time and talents to helping make *The Eastman Theatre: Fulfilling George Eastman's Dream* come true.

Armstrong Grill Staff

Juliana Athayde

Ellen Beck

John Beck

David J. Beinetti

Chris Beyer

Christopher Blair

Stephen Blessman

Amy Blum

G. Sheldon Brayer

Michael Bryant

William Cahn

Dale Chihuly

Mathew Colbert

Kathy Connor

David Peter Coppen

John D'Amanda

Wilfredo Degláns

Dudley Duberry

Julia Figueras

Mike Flannery

Adam Gershwin

Rob Gibson

Andrew Green

Andrew Grossman

James Hamm

Patricia Hamm

Janice Hanson

D. Stanley Hasty

Grant Holcomb

Amy Holowczenko

Kathleen Holt

Donald Hunsberger

Polly Hunsberger

Craig Jensen

Tom Judson

Judith and Steven Katten

Nancy Kauffman

Kathy Murphy Kemp

Rose-Marie Klipstein

Vincent Lenti

Tom Lind

Bobbi Lonobile

Douglas Lowry

Janice Macisak

Nancy Macon

Chuck Mangione

Sid Mear

Barbara Moore

Tom Morris

James Norman

Susan Nurse

Sherri Olenick

Lorene Osborn

Charles Owens

Jonathon Parkes

Antonio Perez

David Perlman

Nicole Philipp

Norm Rockefeller

Dr. Jamal Rossi

Tom Sawyer

Christopher Seaman

Marjorie Searl

Joel Seligman

Mike Spooner

Ron Stackman

Jim Thompson

Jeff Tyzik

Charles Valenza

Eugene Van Voorhis

Karen Ver Steeg

Bill Watson

Nancy Zawacki

Robert Zimmerman

Heidi Zimmermeier

*I*MAGE CREDITS

All photographs by Andy Olenick except as listed below.

ARCHIVAL PHOTOGRAPHS:

Betty Strasenburgh Collection:
138 (below left)

Elizabeth Brayer Collection:
6 (right), 7 (above), 11 (left), 16, 17, 18 (left & middle), 20 (left), 24 (left), 24-25 (middle), 29 (above–middle & right), 36 (left), 40 (above middle), 41 (left), 44, 46, 47 (left & right), 57, 62, 64 (right), 69, 83 (right), 84 (middle right), 90 (above & below), 91 (right), 94 (right), 95 (right–above, middle & below), 117, 119 (right), 127 (above right), 128 (above–far right), 147 (above), 168 (left), 182 (below right)

Eastman School of Music:
35, 95 (above left), 97, 124 (above left & below right), 125 (middle–left & right), 126 (above–far left, middle right & far right; below left), 127 (above–far left; below–left & right), 129 (upper three photographs), 155

George Eastman Legacy Collection, George Eastman House:
6 (left), 7 (photos left & below right, ledger below right), 8, 10, 11 (right), 12 (above–left & right, below right), 13 (left & right), 15 (right), 19 (right), 22 (left), 24 (below), 26 (above middle), 29 (below), 36 (middle & right), 43 (right), 51, 52 (left), 53, 55, 60-61, 70, 71 (left), 79, 83 (above), 84 (below right), 121 (bottom right), 147 (below), 159 (above left), 176 (left), 177 (below left)

Margaret Woodbury Strong Collection, Courtesy of Anne Hotra:
15 (left), 38 (above, bottom left, below right), 121 (above right, below right)

Rochester Philharmonic Orchestra:
140 (middle left and below right), 141 (below left)

Sid Mear Collection:
85 (left), 131 (left & right), 132 (above–left, middle & right), 136 (above right)

Sibley Music Library:
18 (below right), 125 (above left), 133 (above–left & right), 141 (above–far left)

Alexander Leventon Collection *(all photographs by Alexander Leventon): 52 (right), 81 (middle), 118 (middle above), 124 (below left)*

David James Collection: *78 (above right), 134 (above middle), 135 (above–far left & middle right)*

Eastman School of Music Archives: *23, 25 (above right)*
From The Note Book *(The Eastman School of Music publication): 19 (above), 48 (bottom row: left), 49 (top row: right; middle row: left; bottom row: left & middle), 54*

Eastman School Photo Archives: *14 (above), 19 (below left), 21, 39, 40 (middle & below right), 42, 43 (above), 48 (top row: left; middle row: left & right; bottom row: right), 49 (top row: left & middle; middle row: middle & right; bottom row:*

right), 50 (left & right), 58, 71 (right), 72 , 73 (left & right), 74, 76 (above left & right), 77 (all), 80, 81 (left & right), 82 (below right), 98, 99 (above), 118 (below), 119 (above–left, middle & right), 120, 122 (all), 123 (left), 124 (above middle & below–far left), 125 (above–middle & right), 126 (above–middle left), 127 (above–middle left), 132 (below), 133 (above left), 134 (middle & below left), 135 (middle left), 140 (above middle)

Gannett News Photographs Collection:
68, 76 (middle), 78 (above middle), 82 (above–left, middle & right, middle left), 127 (above–middle right), 134 (above–left & right), 135 (above–far right), 136 (above–middle), 141 (above–middle right)

Herman Rudin Collection:
48 (top row: right), 78 (below left, above right), 130 (below)

Louis Ouzer Collection (all photographs by Lou Ouzer):
64 (left), 86 (above & below), 124 (above right), 128 (above middle), 130 (middle below), 135 (above–middle left), 136 (above left), 137 (all), 138 (above–left, middle & right), 139 (above left & right), 140 (above left), 141 (above–middle left), 161

Richard Pearlman Collection:
128 (left)

University of Rochester Library:
9, 12 (below left), 20 (right), 26 (below), 27 (above & below), 28 (all), 30, 31, 38 (middle left), 85 (right), 123 (right)

Department of Rare Books and Special Collections:
159 (middle–left, middle & right)

COURTESY / PERMISSIONS:

14–Photograph of newspaper clipping courtesy of Vincent Lenti

22–Photograph of painting courtesy of Stephen Blessman and Kathy Connor

23–Advertisement reproduced with permission of Austin Organs, Inc.

25–Photograph of musical score reproduced with permission of Adam Gershwin

29–Photograph of William Kaelber: Schmidt, Carl and Ann, Architecture and Architects of Rochester, NY., 1959. Rochester Society of Architects, pg. 73. SUNY Geneseo Collection

35–Maxfield Parrish, Interlude, 1922. Oil on linen canvas, 5.97L. Photograph courtesy of Memorial Art Gallery of the University of Rochester

45–Peter Pan stills courtesy of Paramount Pictures

45–The Snowman movie photograph published with permission of Snowman Enterprises Ltd.

63–Photograph of Martha Graham ©Bettman/Corbis

66-67–Batiste Madalena posters ©Judith and Steven Katten, photograph of Batiste Madalena courtesy of Judith and Steven Katten

84–Photograph of Winston Churchill: American Heritage Magazine and UPI, comp. Churchill the Life Triumphant. American Heritage Publishing Co., Inc.,1965

85, 116–Use of the photographs of portraits by Kathleen McEnery Cunningham courtesy of McEnery-Cunningham family

99–Photograph of Barry Faulkner courtesy of Phil Faulkner

114-115–Psyche and Cupid by Dufour: Reproductions by James Hamm

118–(below) Photograph by Loulen Studio

119–(above middle) Photograph by Linn Duncan Studio

122 (above left), 124 (above middle), 125 (above middle & below left), 126 (above–middle left), 140 (above middle)–Photographs by Lou Ouzer, in addition to those listed above in the Louis Ouzer Collection of the Sibley Music Library

123–(left) Photograph by Loulen Studio

135–Photograph of William L. Cahn by Kent Divers

138–Photograph courtesy of William L. Cahn

140–Photograph of Itzhak Perlman ©Bettman/Corbis

139–Photograph of Mark Elder ©Zoe Dominic

141–Photograph of Jeff Tyzik ©Tyler Boye

141–Photograph of Jessye Norman courtesy of James Norman

141–Photograph of Misha Dichter ©John Russell, courtesy of Shuman Associates

141 (below right), 162–Use of the photographs courtesy of Cirque de la Symphonie

143–Photograph courtesy of William L. Cahn

146, 150, 151, 153–Architectural drawings by Robert Macon, courtesy of Nancy Macon

149–Map graphics ©SWBR Architects

160–Diagram ©Akustiks, courtesy of Christopher Blair

176–Geo signature courtesy of Eastman School of Music

182–Sketch courtesy of Chaintreuil Jensen Stark Architects, LLP

196–(right) Photograph by Pat St. Clair, St. Clair Photo-imaging

197–(below) Rendering courtesy of Chaintreuil Jensen Stark Architects, LLP

Index